STEAMING!

By the same author

Microwave Cooking Times At A Glance!
The Combination Microwave Cook
Microwave Recipes For One
The Blender Book

Uniform with this book

STEAMING!

WITH RECIPES

Annette Yates

RIGHT WAY

Constable & Robinson Ltd
3 The Lanchesters
162 Fulham Palace Road
London W6 9ER
www.right-way.co.uk
www.constablerobinson.com

First published in the UK 2000

This edition published by Right Way, an imprint of
Constable & Robinson, 2008

Copyright © Constable & Robinson 2008

A copy of the British Library Cataloguing in Publication
Data is available from the British Library

ISBN: 978-0-7160-2202-2

Printed and bound in the EU

CONTENTS

ACKNOWLEDGEMENTS

My thanks go to:

TEFAL for supplying me with an electric steamer – their Steam Cuisine 2000 Turbo Diffusion (their contact details appear on page 16).

Dr Sally-Ann Burnett at Canterbury Christ Church University College for answering, in layman's language, some of my queries about nutrient loss in steaming versus boiling.

My husband, Huw, and the rest of my family for their continued enthusiasm in eating the dishes I put in front of them and for giving their honest opinions.

Emma Thomas and Ted French for their excellent illustrations.

INTRODUCING STEAMING

Steaming is a tried-and-tested cooking technique that I am happy to use on a daily basis. As well as being easy, clean and economical, it can also be an asset to eating healthily.

To steam is to cook food in the steam or the vapour given off by boiling water. As a cooking method it can be traced back as far as Neolithic times, particularly in China where the steamer is one of the oldest cooking utensils. To this day, it is still a very popular cooking method in Chinese kitchens, where it is unusual to find an oven. Here in the UK, with the explosion of new cooking appliances and gadgets, steaming did perhaps lose a little of its popularity (though I know there will be many readers who have always made good use of their steamers). With all the advantages steaming has to offer, its current revival is well-deserved.

After all, steaming is a gentle, moist method of cooking that makes the food tender, retains its shape and texture and preserves its colour, all with little chance of the food over-cooking. Food cooked in the steamer takes slightly longer to cook than if it were boiled – so, with that greater margin for error, it's easier to cook vegetables and fish, in particular, to just the right degree of tenderness without overdoing them.

Most of us know that steaming is ideal for cooking vegetables and fish (in school, I remember learning that steamed fish was 'highly suitable' for babies, invalids and the elderly). How many of us, I wonder, would associate steaming with chicken, duck, beef, pork, lamb, rice, couscous, eggs and fruit? As you will discover in the recipes that follow, steaming is great for all these too.

In my tests, steaming has proved to be economical, with several foods cooking in the baskets of a steamer on one burner of the hob, or in the tiers of an electric steamer. This makes it ideal for a range of people and situations, including:

✔ Students and anyone on a limited budget;

✔ People who mostly cook for one or two, or those who need to cook small portions – perhaps for children or for the elderly – and a whole meal can be cooked in the steamer;

✔ Families and cooking for crowds – for example, several vegetables can be cooked in one steamer;

✔ People who need to, or want to, eat food that is easily digestible and low in fat;

✔ Reheating food and keeping food hot for short periods.

There are few problems with flavour transfer from one food to another so, for instance, meat and vegetables can be cooked in the bottom tier while a dessert cooks in the upper tier. I also believe that the natural flavour of food remains more intense during steaming than, say, during boiling or poaching when more flavour is leached into the water. Because the food is cooked in a moist, steamy atmosphere, it is not likely to dry out and toughen.

Nutritionally, steaming can be beneficial too. Research has shown that steaming retains more of the water-soluble vitamins that are normally lost in boiling – in particular, Vitamin C. Of course, in steaming (as in boiling) even fewer nutrients are lost if the juices that drip from the food are used in a sauce or gravy. Another obvious health advantage is that steamed food needs little or no fat to keep it moist or to help it to cook.

Finally, let me stress that this is not a book about health. It is a book on steaming that, I hope, balances healthy, low-fat recipes alongside good, old-fashioned puddings – in fact, all the things that a steamer cooks best. Creating this wide variety of recipes has been the most enjoyable task and has proved just how versatile steaming can be.

Happy steaming!

Annette Yates

PART ONE

GETTING STARTED

1

AT-A-GLANCE GUIDE TO STEAMERS

Steaming works on the principle that steam is allowed to circulate freely around the food and, to accommodate this, steamers have lots of perforations or slats in their layers or tiers.

Steaming Stand in a Large Pan:

This is the most basic method and one that is ideal for savoury and sweet puddings. The food cooks in a covered dish that sits on a steaming stand in boiling water in a large lidded pan.

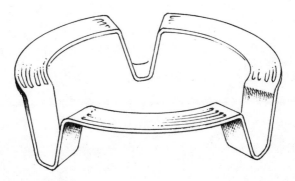

Fig. 1. Steaming stand.

Steaming Baskets

This is an inexpensive way to start enjoying the benefits of steaming by cooking a single layer of food. Probably the most useful type is an expanding perforated metal basket that opens out like the petals of a flower. It is placed in or over a saucepan of boiling liquid and covered with a lid that allows enough space for the steam to circulate around the food.

Fig. 2. Steaming basket.

The second type is a static, colander-type affair, usually made of stainless steel, that fits on top of a saucepan. A universal steamer has a stepped base that enables it to be used on pans of various sizes.

Fig. 3. Universal steamer.

The third type is the Chinese-style bamboo steamer that has a slatted base and close-fitting lid and is available in various diameters. Two or three layers can be stacked one on top of the other, ready for steaming over a wok with boiling water in its base.

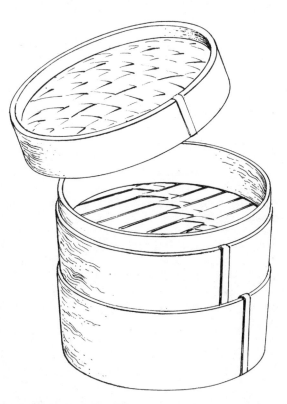

Fig. 4. Bamboo steamer.

Tiered Steamers

These are designed for hob use and usually consist of a stainless steel pan with two steaming tiers (or three at the most – more than this and the steam would not be able to cook the food efficiently). Liquid is boiled in the base to produce the steam that cooks the food in the tiers.

Fig. 5. Tiered steamer.

Multi Cookers

These too are usually stainless steel and are made up of a large pan with a close-fitting, perforated colander that is useful for cooking food in liquid (pasta, for instance). Over this sits a steamer tier, which is then topped with a lid.

Fig. 6. Multi cooker.

Electric Steamers

An electric steamer is designed to stand on the kitchen worktop and plug into a 13 amp socket. A timer automatically switches off the steamer at the end of cooking. Two or three heat-resistant plastic tiers sit on the base, which holds the water, and a thermostatically controlled element heats up the water to create the steam. Some models include a drip tray to catch the food juices, a dish for cooking rice and an area with indents in which to cook eggs in their shells. The advantages of an electric steamer include: the hob is kept free, steam is produced almost instantly, you can see the food inside and, because the bases of the tiers can be removed, a whole chicken or a large piece of meat can be cooked in the resulting 'tube'. It is worth noting that an electric steamer seems to emit more steam through the vents in the lid (it's helpful to position it near an extractor fan) and therefore needs topping up more frequently during long cooking periods.

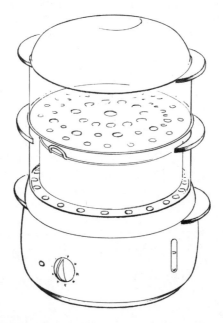

Fig. 7. Electric steamer.

Where to buy steamers and steaming equipment

Lakeland Limited has, at the time of going to print, a selection of steaming equipment in their mail-order catalogue. For details, contact Lakeland Limited, Alexandra Buildings, Windermere, Cumbria LA23 1BQ. Tel: 01539 488100. Fax: 01539 488300. Website: www.lakelandlimited.com

Electric steamers are generally available in department stores. Alternatively, contact TEFAL Customer Relations, PO Box 467, Slough PDO, Berkshire SL3 8WD. Tel: 0845 602 1454 (calls charged at local rate). Fax: 01753 583938. E-mail: customerrelations@tefal.co.uk

2

HOW TO GET THE BEST RESULTS

As with any other method of cooking, using fresh, good-quality ingredients will ensure that you get the best results.

✔ Always check that the **lid** fits securely on the steamer, to keep the steam trapped inside the pan and to cook in the shortest time.

✔ The **water** should be heated to a full rolling boil before adding the food to the steamer.

✔ Make sure there is a **gap** of about 2.5cm/1 in between the food and the liquid in the base of the pan. On no account allow the boiling liquid to come into contact with the food (or it will boil and not steam).

✔ Thoroughly **defrost** foods like fish, poultry and meat before steaming. Frozen vegetables can be steamed from frozen.

✔ Choose **equal-size** pieces of food (such as chicken breasts) to encourage even cooking, and cut foods like vegetables into even-size pieces.

✔ Whenever possible, **arrange** foods in the steamer so that there are gaps between them, to allow the steam to circulate and cook evenly.

- ✔ Arrange food in an **even layer** in the steamer, again to promote evenly-cooked results. The larger the piece or the thicker the layer of food, the longer the cooking time will be.

- ✔ Food such as vegetables, fish, meat and poultry can be placed **directly in the steamer.** To prevent food, such as steamed puddings, becoming too wet, put it in a **covered dish.**

- ✔ Foods that are likely to **drip**, like fish, poultry and meat, should be placed in the bottom tier, so that they do not affect the other foods.

- ✔ Put the food with the **shortest cooking time** in the top tier and, if necessary, add it to the steamer at an appropriate stage during cooking. Food in the top tier is further away from the source of the steam and will take slightly longer to cook.

- ✔ When cooking a **large quantity** of food, it's a good idea to swap the tiers half way through cooking to encourage even cooking.

- ✔ **Cover** foods only when contact with the steam might cause the dish to spoil – for example, steamed puddings. See also the note about covering on page 21.

- ✔ For long periods of cooking, such as for a steamed pudding, you may need to **top up** the water in the base of the steamer by adding boiling water from the kettle. To do this with a hob-type steamer, simply lift the tiers off the pan. If you are steaming on a steaming stand in a large pan, simply add the water through the gap between bowl and pan. Electric steamers usually have a special opening through which you can top up the water – just follow the manufacturer's instructions.

- ✔ **Resist the temptation** to lift the lid and peek into the steamer during cooking. If you do, steam will be lost and the cooking time will be lengthened.

- ✔ **Check that the food is cooked** before serving. With steaming, as with any other method, cooking times will vary according to the quantity and quality of the food. If the food is not cooked to your liking, simply replace the lid and steam for a few minutes longer.

Some Quick and Simple Additions
to Steamed Food

Before steaming, try sprinkling vegetables, fish, poultry or meat with:

★   Lemon, lime or orange juice, wine vinegar or sherry vinegar;

★   Finely grated citrus zest – lemon or lime;

★   Chopped fresh herbs;

★   Finely chopped or crushed garlic;

★   Finely chopped fresh root ginger;

★   Fresh root ginger juice – take a handful of roughly grated root ginger (skin and all) and squeeze tightly so that the delicately-flavoured juice runs from it;

★   Ground spices (particularly freshly ground) – such as coriander, cumin, chilli, cinnamon, allspice, cloves or nutmeg;

★   Shallots or mild red or white onion, finely chopped or thinly sliced;

★   Good quality oil, such as olive, sesame or walnut.

3

RECIPE NOTES

All the recipes in this book have been tested successfully in a tiered steamer on the hob and, with the exception of the pasta dishes (pages 57 – 60), in an electric steamer.

Servings: you will see that the majority of recipes have been developed to serve two. There are several reasons for this. Firstly many of you, I know, cook most frequently for two. Secondly, some recipes that serve two actually fill the steamer and, thirdly, I always think it's easier to multiply a recipe than it is to reduce it. Having said all this, some recipes seem ultimately more appropriate for feeding four or more people – in which case they do! And I hope you will forgive such quirks.

Ingredients are listed in both metric and imperial. You will notice that the metric versions give quantities that are easier to measure. Now that we buy our foods in metric quantities, it seems a good idea to wean ourselves (and that includes me) off imperial measurements with the aim of moving over to metric only. It would be so much simpler for all of us and it's really quite easy. In the meantime, imperial measures are listed, though you may find them slightly more awkward to use.

Spoon measurements are always level unless otherwise stated.

Eggs are usually medium, unless otherwise stated. Some recipes may contain eggs that are cooked only until they are soft or just set. Do remember that we are advised not to serve undercooked eggs to pregnant women, the elderly, the very young or the sick.

Fat, where possible, is kept to a minimum in the recipes. Very often it is included to add flavour and to improve the texture. However, there may be some dishes where you might want to reduce the amount of fat further, by omitting the oil perhaps, and that's fine.

Sugar, in very small amounts, is used in some recipes as a seasoning, to bring out the flavour of the other ingredients.

Recipe methods – I like to keep the recipes as simple as possible to prepare and in this book I have tried to avoid pre-cooking food before it goes in the steamer (unless of course it is essential to the final colour, texture or flavour of the dish). After all, there is little point in extolling the ease of use and cleanliness of the steamer, if you have to clean up several extra pans along the way.

Covering: One thing that used to put me off the idea of steaming (and puddings in particular) was the laborious process of covering dishes – first with greased and pleated greaseproof paper and secondly with pleated foil. These were then tied on with string and a string handle attached for easy removal of the hot dish from the steamer. Nothing wrong with any of this, it's true, and if you are happy with the method, then please carry on using it. However, nowadays I simply cover the dish, first with baking paper (it's non stick so there is no need to grease it) and then with a large square of foil, and crimp and scrunch the edges, pressing them firmly against the sides of the dish. Admittedly you will need to use an oven cloth to lift the dish from the steamer, but if you are in a hurry at the time this is a good method.

4

COOKING CHARTS

These cooking times are provided as a guide only – they will depend on the quantity and quality of the foods to be steamed and, of course, on your personal taste.

EGGS – 1-6	COOKING TIME	COMMENTS
Whole, in shells: **Soft 'boiled'** **Hard 'boiled'**	8-10 minutes. 10-18 minutes.	The short cooking times are for 1 egg, the longer times are for 6 eggs.
In small dish or ramekin: **Soft** **Hard**	5-10 minutes. 10-15 minutes.	The short cooking times are for 1 egg, the longer times are for 6 eggs.

VEGETABLES – about 250g/9 oz	COOKING TIME	COMMENTS
Frozen vegetables need not be defrosted before steaming. Just allow a few minutes longer cooking time. Avoid strong-flavoured vegetables such as kale or mustard greens – they are likely to transfer their flavour to other foods.		
Artichokes – Globe	30-45 minutes or until the base is tender.	Before cooking, cut off the base so the artichoke sits level in the steamer.
Artichokes – Jerusalem, whole	About 20 minutes.	For the best flavour, leave the skins on during steaming (prick them first).

Asparagus	10-15 minutes.	Arrange the stalks so that they cross over each other – to allow the steam to circulate. Take care not to overcook or the quick-cooking tips will be too soft.
Beans – Green	10-15 minutes.	Arrange the beans so that they cross over each other – to allow the steam to circulate.
Beans – Runner, sliced	10-15 minutes.	
Broccoli	10-15 minutes.	
Brussels Sprouts	15-20 minutes.	Once cooked, try mashing them with a knob of butter and a good grating of fresh nutmeg.
Cabbage, quartered	About 40 minutes.	
sliced or shredded	About 15 minutes.	
Carrots, sliced or cut into matchsticks	About 20 minutes.	
whole	30-45 minutes.	
Cauliflower florets	10-15 minutes.	
Celeriac, cut into cubes or slices	About 20 minutes.	Sprinkling the uncooked celeriac with a little lemon juice helps to keep its colour.
Chinese Leaves, roughly chopped	About 2 minutes.	Once cooked, toss with a little soy or oyster sauce.
Corn – Dwarf	About 10 minutes.	
Corn on the cob	About 30 minutes.	Season with salt after cooking or the skins will toughen.

Courgettes, small whole	5-10 minutes.	Take care not to overcook them or they will become watery.
sliced	About 5 minutes.	
Garlic, whole cloves	About 10 minutes.	Once cooked, squeeze the garlic out of its paper-like casing.
Garlic – Wild	5-10 minutes.	For leaves that are just wilted, cook for a very short time.
Leeks, small whole or sliced	20-25 minutes.	
Mange Tout	5-10 minutes.	Cook until they still have a slight 'bite'.
Mushrooms	About 5 minutes.	
Onions, small whole	15-20 minutes.	
sliced	10-15 minutes.	
Pak Choi, roughly chopped	About 2 minutes.	Once cooked, toss with a little soy or oyster sauce
Parsnip, sliced or cut into cubes	30-45 minutes.	Once cooked, leave whole or mash until smooth.
Peas, fresh	8-12 minutes.	
Peppers, seeds removed and cut into wide strips	About 10 minutes.	
Potatoes, small whole or cut into cubes	About 20 minutes.	
Seakale, shredded	20-25 minutes.	
Spinach	5-10 minutes.	For leaves that are just wilted, cook for a very short time.
Squash, seeds removed and cut into wedges or peeled and cut into cubes	20-30 minutes.	Once cooked, serve just as it is or mash until smooth and stir in some cream and ground cinnamon or nutmeg.

Swede, sliced or cubed	30-45 minutes.	Once cooked, leave whole or mash until smooth.

COUSCOUS, BULGAR AND RICE	QUANTITY	COOKING TIME
The liquid used could be water or stock with some wine or fruit juice. Put the couscous, bulgar or rice into a container with the liquid and steam uncovered.		
Couscous	200g/7 oz plus 400ml/14 fl oz liquid.	10 minutes.
Bulgar (or cracked) wheat	200g/7 oz plus 400ml/14 fl oz liquid.	20-25 minutes.
Rice – Long grain white	200g/7 oz plus 400ml/14 fl oz liquid.	About 25 minutes.
Brown	200g/7 oz plus 450ml/16 fl oz liquid.	About 35 minutes.

FISH – 250-500g/ 9 oz-1 lb 2 oz	COOKING TIME	COMMENTS
Frozen fish need not be thawed before steaming but will probably take longer to cook.		
Thin fillets: cod, haddock, plaice, sole, salmon, etc	5-10 minutes.	Placing them on baking paper makes them easier to remove from the steamer.
Thick fillets or steaks: cod, haddock, monkfish, salmon, tuna, sword fish, etc	10-15 minutes.	
Whole fish: trout, salmon trout, bass, mullet, red snapper, etc	15-20 minutes.	Placing the fish on baking paper makes for easy removal from the steamer.
Clams, cockles	About 5 minutes, until the shells have opened.	Stir half way. Once cooked, discard any unopened shells.
Lobster tails, fresh frozen	About 15 minutes. About 20 minutes.	

Mussels	5-10 minutes, or until the shells have opened.	Stir half way. Once cooked, discard any unopened shells.
Oysters, in shells	About 5 minutes, until the shells open easily.	
Prawns	About 5 minutes, until raw prawns turn pink or cooked prawns are just hot.	Stir half way.
Scallops	About 5 minutes, until just set.	Re-arrange half way.

POULTRY AND MEAT – 250-500g/ 9 oz-1 lb 2 oz	COOKING TIME	COMMENTS
Thoroughly defrost all poultry and meat before cooking.		
Chicken – Boneless breasts Joints	12-15 minutes. About 30 minutes.	The juices should run clear (not pink) when the thickest part of the chicken is pierced with a skewer.
Duck breasts	25-30 minutes.	The skin can be removed before or after cooking.
Lamb neck fillet, cut in 1cm/½ in slices	About 15 minutes.	
Pork fillet, cut in 1cm/½ in slices	About 15 minutes.	
Frankfurters and smoked sausages	10-15 minutes.	Prick before steaming.

FRUIT	COOKING TIME	COMMENTS
To catch the juices from the fruit, line the steamer with a sheet of baking paper or foil.		
Apples – Whole, peeled Cored and quartered	About 20 minutes. About 10 minutes.	Rub a little lemon juice over the cut surface.

Apricots – Whole or halved	5-10 minutes.	Prick whole apricots before steaming.
Bananas	12-15 minutes, until the skins are brown and just beginning to split open.	See recipe, page 117.
Nectarines – Whole or halved	15-20 minutes.	Prick whole nectarines before steaming.
Peaches – Whole or halved	15-20 minutes.	Prick whole peaches before steaming.
Pears – Ripe, whole, peeled	About 20 minutes.	Rub a little lemon juice over the cut surface.
Plums – Whole or halved	5-10 minutes.	Prick whole plums before steaming.
Rhubarb, cut into 2.5cm/1 in lengths	5-10 minutes.	

PART TWO

RECIPES

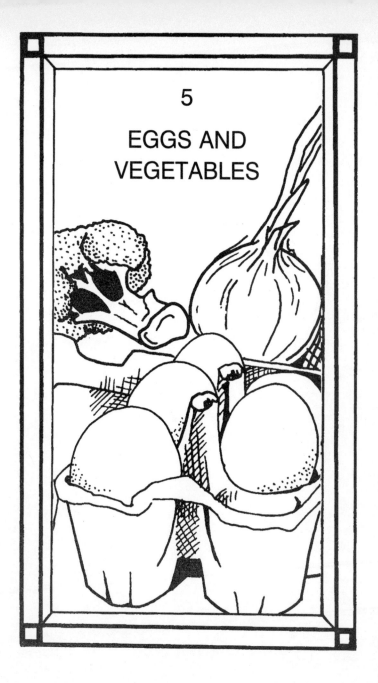

5

EGGS AND VEGETABLES

Eggs in Dishes with Cream and Herbs

This is a quick and easy lunch dish or starter, ideal for serving with crisp fingers of toast.

Serves 2

butter
2 eggs
salt and freshly ground black pepper
2 tbsp double or soured cream
1 tbsp chopped fresh herbs, such as parsley or coriander
paprika

1. Lightly butter two small dishes or ramekins and crack an egg into each. Season with salt and pepper and spoon the cream over the top. Sprinkle with the herbs and a little paprika.

2. Put the dishes in the steamer and cover with the lid. Steam for 6-10 minutes or until the eggs are set to your taste.

Eggs with Pancetta

Make the recipe above, first lining the dishes with wafer-thin slices of pancetta or Parma ham.

Eggs with Smoked Salmon

Here is another quick and easy lunch dish or starter that is sure to impress your friends. I like to serve it with thin slices of warm Italian bread such as Ciabatta.

Serves 4

butter
4 smoked salmon slices
4 eggs
salt and freshly ground black pepper
4 tbsp double cream
1 tbsp chopped fresh chives

1. Lightly butter four small dishes or ramekins. Chop the salmon and arrange in the base of each dish. Crack an egg into each. Season with salt and pepper, spoon the cream over the top and sprinkle with the chives.

2. Put the dishes in the steamer and cover with the lid. Steam for 8-10 minutes or until the eggs are set to your taste.

Sweet Peppers with Ham and Eggs

These make a filling lunch or supper served with crusty bread. I like the peppers to have a slight 'bite' but, if you prefer them soft, just steam them for an extra 2-3 minutes in step 2.

Serves 2

2 medium red peppers
2 tsp pesto sauce
2 thin slices of smoked ham
4 medium eggs
salt and freshly ground black pepper

1. Halve the peppers lengthways, removing the seeds but leaving the stalks intact.

2. Place the peppers in a steamer tier, cut side down, and steam for about 5 minutes.

3. Carefully lift the tier off the steamer base and turn the peppers over so that they sit cut side up. Put ½ tsp pesto sauce in each pepper half. Halve the ham slices and press one piece into each pepper (you may need to tear the ham to make room for the eggs). Crack the eggs on to the ham and top with a seasoning of salt and pepper.

4. Replace the steamer tier on the base pan and cover with the lid. Steam for 6-10 minutes or until the eggs are set to your liking.

Courgette and Mint Timbales

These vegetable moulds can be served warm, though I think the flavour is even better after they have been chilled overnight. Their light texture allows them to be served just as they are, with crusty bread or crisp biscuits. Alternatively, serve them with buttered new potatoes and salad accompaniments – such as sliced tomatoes with olives, or baby green leaves with thin rings of red onion.

Serves 4 as a starter, 2 as a main course

300g/10½ oz small courgettes
1 tbsp oil
1 small onion, finely chopped
1 garlic clove, crushed
1 tbsp finely chopped fresh mint or 1 tsp dried
250g carton of curd cheese
1 large egg
40g/1½ oz fresh white breadcrumbs
salt and freshly ground black pepper

1. From one courgette, cut 16 very thin slices (crossways) and put them into a colander. Pour over boiling water (from the kettle) and leave them to drain. Roughly chop the remaining courgettes.
2. Lightly oil four small dishes or ramekins. Pat the courgette slices dry and arrange them, overlapping, in the base of the dishes.
3. Heat the oil in a non-stick pan and add the onion and garlic. Cook over medium heat for about 5 minutes, stirring occasionally, until the onion is soft but not brown. Add the chopped courgettes and the mint. Cover and cook for about 5 minutes, stirring once or twice until the courgettes are just soft.
4. Tip the curd cheese into a food processor and add the egg. Blend until smooth. Add the courgette mixture and any juices, the breadcrumbs and a generous seasoning of salt and pepper. Blend until evenly mixed.
5. Spoon the mixture into the prepared dishes and level the top. Cover with baking paper and then foil, crimping the edges securely against the sides of the dishes.
6. Put the dishes in the steamer and cover with the lid. Steam for 20 minutes.
7. Leave in their dishes for 5-10 minutes before turning out.

Corn on the Cob with Onion and Herb Butter

This easy lunch dish is a favourite with my nieces when they visit during the summer holidays. The method works well with frozen corn too.

Serves 2

2 corn on the cob, husks removed
50g/1¾ oz soft butter
4 spring onions, chopped
1 tbsp finely chopped fresh parsley
leaves from 1 fresh rosemary sprig
salt and freshly ground black pepper

1. Put the corn in the bottom tier of the steamer and cover with the lid. Steam for 15 minutes.

2. Meanwhile, put the butter into a bowl that will fit into the steamer. Add the onions, parsley and rosemary leaves. Season lightly with salt and pepper. Cover the dish with foil, crimping the edges securely to the sides of the dish.

3. Put the dish in the second tier, add it to the steamer and cover with the lid. Steam for a further 15 minutes or until the corn is tender.

4. To serve, season the corn with salt and pepper to taste, stir the buttery juices and pour over the corn.

Squash Parcels with Brown Sugar and Cinnamon

Squash cooks beautifully in the steamer to a smooth, creamy texture. Some delicious juices collect in the parcels – just mash the squash into them as you eat. Try other types of squash too – such as the yellow-fleshed butternut. I like to serve this as an accompaniment to grilled meat or fish, or just as it is with a sprinkling of freshly grated Parmesan cheese.

Serves 4

1 small acorn squash
4 tsp muscovado sugar
½ tsp ground cinnamon
100g/3½ oz butter
4 tsp lemon juice or white wine, cider or sherry vinegar
2 tbsp finely chopped fresh herb, such as parsley, basil or coriander
salt and freshly ground black pepper

1. Cut the squash into quarters and scoop out and discard the seeds and membranes. Remove the skin and cut into bite-size cubes.

2. Divide the squash (in even layers) between four squares of foil or baking paper, each large enough to enclose it completely. Mix together the sugar and cinnamon and sprinkle on the squash. Top each with one quarter of the butter, lemon juice, herbs and seasoning. Close the parcels, securing the seams well.

3. Put the parcels in the steamer and cover with the lid. Steam for about 30 minutes or until the squash is soft and tender.

Baby Vegetables with Lime and Pesto

This is a recipe that I created originally for cooking on the barbecue. It suits the steamer perfectly too. These parcels of baby vegetables go particularly well with grilled fish or chicken.

Serves 4

450g/1 lb mixed small vegetables, such as sugar snap peas, asparagus tips, baby sweetcorn and cherry tomatoes
1 small lime, quartered
4 tsp pesto sauce
4 tsp dry white vermouth or wine
2 sun-dried tomatoes in oil, drained and cut into thin slivers (not essential but delicious)
salt and freshly ground black pepper

1. Arrange the mixed vegetables on four squares of baking paper or foil, each large enough to enclose them completely. Top each pile of vegetables with one quarter of the lime, pesto sauce and vermouth. Add the sun-dried tomatoes. Season lightly with salt and pepper. Close the parcels, securing the edges well.

2. Put the parcels in the steamer and cover with the lid. Steam for about 10 minutes or until the vegetables are tender yet still slightly crisp.

Peppers Stuffed with Aubergine, Courgette and Ham

For a spicier version, add a finely chopped red or green chilli to the stuffing mixture.

Serves 4 as a starter, 2 as a main dish

2 large red or yellow peppers, or one of each
2 tbsp olive oil
1 small onion, finely chopped
1 garlic clove, crushed
1 aubergine, weighing about 225g/8 oz, chopped
1 medium courgette, chopped
3 tbsp tomato purée
3 tbsp dry white vermouth or wine
salt and freshly ground black pepper
85g/3 oz smoked ham, finely chopped
1 tbsp finely chopped fresh parsley
4 tsp freshly grated Parmesan cheese

1. Halve the peppers lengthways, cutting through the stem. Remove all seeds and white membranes, leaving the stems intact.

2. Heat the oil in a non-stick frying pan. Add the onion and garlic and cook over medium heat for about 5 minutes, stirring occasionally, until soft but not brown. Stir in the aubergine and courgette. Cook over medium heat for about 10 minutes, stirring occasionally, or until the vegetables are tender and beginning to turn golden brown.

3. Stir the tomato purée into the vermouth and add to the vegetables in the pan. Season to taste with salt and pepper. Remove from the heat and stir in the ham.

4. Fill the pepper halves with the vegetable mixture, pressing it in lightly.

5. Stand the peppers in one or two steamer tiers. Cover with the lid and steam for about 20 minutes or until the peppers are soft.

6. To serve, combine the parsley and Parmesan cheese and scatter over the top.

New Potato and Green Bean Salad

Cooked vegetable salads are easy to make with a steamer because you can cook small amounts of several vegetables at once. Here, I have combined baby new potatoes with green beans. Serve it hot or at room temperature. The dressing is just as delicious stirred into a mixture of freshly cooked baby vegetables, such as carrots, courgettes, asparagus and sugar snap peas.

Serves 4-6

675g/1½ lb small new potatoes, scrubbed
225g/8 oz green beans, halved crossways
4 eggs

Dressing:
2 tbsp red or white wine vinegar
1 garlic clove, crushed
1 tbsp wholegrain mustard
1 tbsp clear honey
4 tbsp olive oil
salt and freshly ground black pepper
1 bunch of spring onions, thinly sliced

1. Make the dressing. Put the vinegar and garlic into a large screw-top jar and shake until mixed. Add the mustard, honey, oil and seasoning and shake until thickened. Add the onions and shake again.
2. Put the potatoes in the bottom steamer tier, cover with the lid and steam for 5 minutes.
3. Put the beans and whole eggs (in their shells) in the second tier, add to the steamer and cover with the lid. Steam for a further 15 minutes or until the vegetables are tender.
4. Put the eggs under cold running water while you tip the potatoes and beans into a large serving bowl. Pour the dressing over the hot vegetables and toss carefully.
5. To serve hot, shell the eggs, cut them into quarters and arrange on top of the potato and bean salad. To serve at room temperature, leave the eggs and salad to cool. Just before serving, shell the eggs, cut them into quarters and arrange on top of the salad.

Spiced Cauliflower Salad

Serve this salad warm or, even better, at room temperature after it has been left to marinate for several hours.

Serves 3-4

1 medium cauliflower, cut into florets
3 tbsp oil
4 tsp white wine vinegar
1 tsp ground coriander
½ tsp ground cumin
½ tsp ground turmeric
1 tbsp apricot jam
2 tbsp double cream
2 tbsp finely chopped fresh herbs, such as parsley or thyme
salt and freshly ground black pepper
25g/1 oz toasted flaked almonds

1. Arrange the cauliflower florets in a steamer tier.

2. Put the oil, vinegar, spices and jam into a small dish that will fit alongside the cauliflower. Stir well, then cover with foil, crimping the edges securely against the sides of the dish. Stand the dish alongside the cauliflower.

3. Cover with the lid and steam for about 10 minutes or until the cauliflower still has a slight bite.

4. Tip the cauliflower into a large bowl. Stir the cream and herbs into the hot dressing and season with salt and pepper. Pour the dressing over the hot cauliflower and toss gently until coated.

5. Just before serving, scatter the almonds over the top.

Baby Onions with Parsley and Lemon Butter

This is a great way to cook onions as an accompaniment – you could cook the main dish in another tier. Flat-leaf parsley is better than the curly variety for this recipe. Garlic lovers should try adding several whole (peeled) garlic cloves to the packet in step 2.

Serves 4

350g/12 oz small onions
salt and freshly ground black pepper
2 tsp lemon juice
paprika
50g/1¾ oz butter
2 tbsp finely chopped fresh parsley

1. To peel the onions, put them into a bowl and cover with boiling water (from the kettle). Leave to stand for 5 minutes, after which the skins will be easy to remove with a sharp knife.

2. Put the onions into a steamer tier lined with a square of baking paper or foil, large enough to enclose them completely. Season lightly with salt and generously with pepper. Sprinkle the lemon juice over and dust with a little paprika. Cut the butter into pieces and dot over the onions. Scatter the parsley over the top.

3. Seal the parcel securely.

4. Assemble the steamer and cover with the lid. Steam for about 30 minutes or until the onions are very soft.

Baby Carrots and Petits Pois in a Creamy Mint Sauce

Like the last recipe, the vegetables can be cooked on one tier while the main course cooks on another. This dish looks really pretty if the carrots have some stalk left on them.

Serves 4

225g/8 oz baby carrots, halved lengthways
salt and freshly ground black pepper
100g/3½ oz frozen petits pois
2 tsp clear honey
4 tbsp crème fraîche
2 tbsp finely chopped fresh mint leaves

1.   Put the carrots into a steamer tier. Season lightly with salt and generously with pepper.

2.   Put the petits pois into a dish that will sit alongside the carrots. Add the honey, crème fraîche and mint. Cover with foil, crimping the edges securely to the sides of the dish.

3.   Put the dish alongside the carrots, assemble the steamer and cover with the lid.

4.   Steam for about 20 minutes or until the carrots are just tender.

5.   To serve, tip the carrots into a serving dish, Stir the crème fraîche mixture and pour over.

Lentil Dhal

Though steaming seems like an odd method for cooking dhal, it's quite convenient because you need pay little attention to it while its flavour develops and there is no sticky pan to wash up. I like quite a chunky dhal but, if you prefer it smoother, simply pop the cooked mixture in the food processor and blend for a few seconds. Serve as it is with freshly cooked rice or to accompany spicy foods.

Serves 2

1 tbsp oil
1 medium red onion, finely chopped
2 garlic cloves, crushed
100g/3½ oz red lentils
300ml/½ pt hot vegetable stock
finely grated rind and juice of 1 small lemon
2 tsp sugar
1 tsp grated fresh root ginger
½ tsp ground cumin
¼ tsp turmeric
¼ tsp chilli powder
salt and freshly ground black pepper
plenty of chopped fresh coriander, to serve

1. Put the oil into a bowl that will fit in the steamer. Stir in the onion, garlic and lentils, then pour over the hot stock. Stir in the lemon rind and juice, sugar, ginger, spices and seasoning.

2. Put the uncovered bowl into the steamer. Cover with the lid and steam for about 1 hour, stirring half way, or until the lentils are soft.

3. To serve, stir in a generous quantity of coriander.

Mushroom and Cheese Pots

Serve these warm as a starter or as a delicious light meal with crusty bread or slices of hot toast.

Serves 4

15g/½ oz butter
1 small onion, finely chopped
225g/8 oz cup mushrooms, sliced
1 medium egg
6 tbsp crème fraîche
1 tbsp chopped fresh parsley or thyme, plus extra for garnish
salt and freshly ground black pepper
100g/3¾ oz mature Cheddar cheese, grated

1. Melt the butter in a non-stick pan and cook the onion and mushrooms for about 5 minutes, stirring frequently, until very soft but not brown.

2. Lightly beat the egg and stir in the crème fraîche and herb. Season with salt and pepper.

3. Divide the mushroom mixture between four small dishes or ramekins and sprinkle the cheese over the top. Spoon the egg mixture over the cheese.

4. Cover the dishes with foil, crimping the edges securely against the sides of the dishes.

5. Put the dishes in the steamer and cover with the lid. Steam for 15-20 minutes until set.

6. Serve, sprinkled with extra chopped herb.

Herbed Couscous Stuffed Peppers

This makes a lovely lunch, served warm or at room temperature on a bed of dressed salad leaves with a few black olives. I prefer to use red, yellow or orange peppers because they are sweeter than the green ones. Sometimes I add some toasted pine nuts, chopped anchovies or capers to the couscous stuffing.

Serves 4

175g/6 oz couscous
300ml/½ pt hot vegetable stock
1 tsp ground mixed spice
2 tbsp olive oil
1 tbsp wine vinegar or lemon juice
4 spring onions, thinly sliced
3 tbsp finely chopped fresh parsley
3 tbsp finely chopped fresh mint
salt and freshly ground black pepper
4 medium red, yellow or orange peppers

1. Put the couscous into a large bowl, pour over the hot vegetable stock and stir in the mixed spice. Leave to stand for about 5 minutes or until the stock has been absorbed. Stir in the oil, vinegar, onions, herbs and seasoning to taste.

2. Cut the tops off the peppers and discard. Scrape out and discard the seeds and white membrane. Spoon the couscous mixture into the peppers, pressing it in lightly, and stand them in a steamer tier. (You may need to trim a little off the bottom of each pepper in order to make them stand upright – but try not to cut right through to the filling.)

3. Place the steamer tier on the base pan and cover with the lid. Steam for about 20 minutes or until the peppers are just soft.

Champ

This traditional Irish dish is also known as thump. It goes well with grilled fish, meat or sausages.

Serves 2 as a light meal, 4 as an accompaniment

500g/1 lb 2 oz floury potatoes, such as King Edward or Desirée, weighed after peeling and cutting into chunks
150ml/¼ pt milk
1 bunch of spring onions, thinly sliced
salt and freshly ground black pepper
butter

1. Put the potatoes in the bottom steamer tier.

2. Put the milk and onions into a bowl that will fit the steamer. Cover with foil, crimping the edges securely against the sides of the bowl. Place the bowl in the second tier. Assemble the steamer and cover with the lid.

3. Steam for about 20 minutes or until the potatoes are tender.

4. Tip the potatoes into a large bowl and mash. Beat in the hot milk and onions and seasoning to taste. The mixture should be light and fluffy.

5. Serve, piled on to plates, with a large knob of butter on the top.

6

COUSCOUS, BULGAR
RICE AND PASTA

Couscous with Pimientos and Black Olives

This is one of the quickest dishes I make. For flavour, I use black olives with their stones left in but you can of course use the pitted variety. Serve as an accompaniment to grilled fish or meat or as part of a vegetarian spread. Any left over can be cooled and served as a salad, with a spoonful or two of oil-and-vinegar dressing stirred in.

Serves 4

250g/9 oz couscous
400ml/14 fl oz boiling vegetable stock
¼ tsp salt
freshly ground black pepper
1 tbsp olive oil, plus extra if needed
160g jar oven-roasted sweet red peppers (pimientos), drained and thinly sliced into strips
about 20 black olives
2 generous tbsp chopped chives

1. Put the couscous into a bowl that will fit into the steamer and stir in the hot stock, salt, a few grindings of black pepper and 1 tbsp oil. Leave to stand for 5 minutes.

2. Stir in the pepper strips.

3. Put the uncovered bowl into the steamer and cover with the lid. Steam for 10 minutes.

4. Turn the couscous into a large, warmed serving bowl and fluff up with a fork. Stir in the olives and chives and a little extra olive oil to moisten the mixture if wished.

Risotto Rice with Leek, Courgette and Asparagus

Although this dish cannot truthfully be called a risotto, it is similar and just as delicious. Stirring it half way through cooking will encourage a creamy texture.

Serves 2

225g/8 oz risotto rice, such as arborio
1 tbsp olive oil
1 medium leek, thinly sliced
450ml/16 fl oz hot chicken or vegetable stock, plus extra if necessary
1 medium courgette
100g/3½ oz asparagus tips
salt and freshly ground black pepper
25g/1 oz butter
2 tbsp freshly grated Parmesan cheese (optional)

1. Put the rice into a bowl that will fit into the steamer and stir in the oil until well coated. Add the leek, pour over the hot stock and stir well.

2. Put the uncovered bowl into the steamer and cover with the lid. Steam for about 30 minutes, stirring well half way, or until the rice is just tender (still with a slight 'bite') and almost all the liquid has been absorbed.

3. Meanwhile, quarter the courgette lengthways and cut into small pieces. Halve the asparagus tips crossways.

4. After 30 minutes' cooking, season the rice mixture to taste with salt and pepper. At this stage, if the mixture seems to be too dry, add a little extra hot stock. Arrange the courgette and asparagus on top of the rice, cover with the lid and steam for a further 5 minutes.

5. Stir in the butter and Parmesan, if using, and serve immediately.

Spiced Couscous with Apricots and Pine Nuts

The mixture of ingredients in this recipe produces a dish that has a feel and flavour of the Middle East. You will need a small, non-stick frying pan to brown the onion and pine nuts. Serve it as an accompaniment to meat (it is particularly good with lamb), chicken or fish, or as part of a salad table.

Serves 4

1 tbsp olive oil, plus extra if necessary
1 medium onion, finely chopped
2 tsp clear honey
50g/1¾ oz pine nuts
200g/7 oz couscous
1 level tsp ground mixed spice
1 garlic clove, crushed
350ml/12 fl oz hot vegetable stock
100g/3½ oz ready-to-eat dried apricots, cut into slivers
salt and freshly ground black pepper

1. Heat the oil in a small, non-stick frying pan and add the onion and honey. Cook over medium heat for about 5 minutes, stirring occasionally, until soft but not brown. Add the pine nuts, turn up the heat and cook for a few minutes, stirring occasionally until the onion and pine nuts are golden brown.

2. Meanwhile, put the couscous into a bowl that will fit in the steamer. Stir in the spice, garlic, hot stock and apricots. Leave to stand for 5 minutes.

3. Stir the browned onion and pine nuts into the couscous. Season to taste with salt and pepper.

4. Put the uncovered bowl into the steamer and cover with the lid. Steam for 10 minutes.

5. To serve, tip into a warm serving bowl and fluff up with a fork, stirring in a little extra oil if wished.

Bulgar Wheat with Herbs and Lemon

Bulgar, or cracked, wheat has a texture that is firmer than couscous and it tastes almost 'nutty'. Serve this dish as an accompaniment – it goes particularly well with lamb cooked in a sauce – or as part of a buffet. I also like to serve it for lunch, warm or cold, with some oil-and-vinegar dressing stirred into it and some cherry tomatoes and crusty bread alongside.

Serves 4-6

2 tbsp olive oil
250g/9 oz bulgar or cracked wheat
1 medium red onion, finely chopped
500ml/18 fl oz hot vegetable stock
1 tbsp finely chopped fresh mint or 1 tsp dried
1 tbsp finely chopped fresh oregano or thyme leaves, or 1 tsp dried
25g/1 oz sultanas
1 lemon
salt and freshly ground black pepper

1. Put the oil into a bowl that will fit in the steamer. Stir in the bulgar wheat and onion. Pour over the hot stock, add the herbs and sultanas and stir well. Leave to stand for 10 minutes.

2. Finely grate the rind and squeeze the juice from half the lemon (reserve the other half for serving). Add rind and juice to the bulgar wheat and season with salt and pepper.

3. Put the uncovered bowl into the steamer and cover with the lid. Steam for 20-25 minutes or until the bulgar wheat is tender, stirring half way.

4. Tip into a large, warm serving bowl and fluff up with a fork. Cut the reserved lemon into wedges and arrange on top.

Saffron Rice with Two Sorts of Peas

I love the distinctive flavour of rice cooked with saffron. This dish is quite filling so it's good served on its own, perhaps topped with some grated cheese, or with fish, meat or chicken in a sauce.

Serves 4

1 tbsp oil
150g/5½ oz long grain rice
420g can chick peas, drained
pinch of saffron strands
1 good-quality vegetable stock cube
1 tbsp tomato purée
1 garlic clove, crushed
salt and freshly ground black pepper
100g/3½ oz frozen petits pois

1. Put the oil into a bowl that will fit the steamer and stir in the rice until well coated. Stir in the chick peas.

2. Put the saffron and stock cube into a measuring jug and pour over 350ml/12 fl oz boiling water (from the kettle). Stir until the stock cube has dissolved. Stir in the tomato purée and the garlic. Pour the mixture over the rice, season with salt and pepper and stir well.

3. Put the uncovered dish into the steamer and cover with the lid. Steam for about 25 minutes or until the rice is just tender, stirring half way.

4. Scatter the frozen petits pois evenly on top of the rice and continue steaming for a further 5 minutes.

5. Tip the mixture into a large, warm serving bowl and fluff up with a fork, mixing well.

Creamy Porridge

An odd way to cook porridge? Not at all! The result is creamy and there's no sticky 'burnt-on' pan to wash up.

Serves 2

50g/1¾ oz porridge oats
300ml/½ pt full cream milk
salt, sugar or honey

1. Put the oats in a bowl that will fit the steamer (the porridge will boil up slightly in the dish, so choose a fairly deep one) and stir in the milk.

2. Put the uncovered bowl into the steamer and cover with the lid. Steam for about 15 minutes, stirring half way, until thick and creamy.

3. Serve with salt, sugar or honey to taste.

Pasta with Chicken and Crème Fraîche Sauce

A substantial meal, the pasta is cooked in the main pan while the chicken, vegetables and sauce cook in the tiers above.

Serves 2

2 boneless chicken breasts, skinned
2 medium leeks, thinly sliced
2 small carrots, thinly sliced
4 tbsp crème fraîche
1 good-quality chicken stock cube, finely chopped
salt and freshly ground black pepper
200g/7 oz pasta shapes, such as penne or twists
some torn basil leaves

1. Put the chicken in the bottom steamer tier.

2. Put the vegetables in the second tier.

3. Into a small bowl that will fit alongside the vegetables, put the crème fraîche and the stock cube. Stir in 6 tbsp water and season with pepper. Cover with foil, crimping the edges securely to the sides of the dish. Sit the dish beside the vegetables.

4. Pour water in the base of the steamer, sufficient to cover the pasta but not so much that it will boil up into the first tier, and add salt. Bring to a rolling boil and stir in the pasta. When the water returns to the boil, stir the pasta, then assemble the steamer.

5. Cover with the lid and steam for about 12 minutes or for the cooking time given on the pasta packet, until the pasta is just tender and the chicken is cooked through (when pierced with a skewer, the chicken juices should run clear).

6. Drain the pasta thoroughly and tip into warmed serving bowls. Spoon the vegetables on top. Slice the chicken diagonally and arrange it on the vegetables. Stir the sauce and spoon it over the top. Sprinkle the basil over and serve immediately.

Pasta with Peppers and Garlic and Herb Sauce

Here is a simple recipe that is quick and easy to prepare. It's a regular standby in my kitchen.

Serves 2

1 red pepper, seeds removed and cut into strips
1 yellow pepper, seeds removed and cut into strips
125g packet soft cheese with garlic and herb
100ml/3½ fl oz vegetable stock
salt and freshly ground black pepper
200g/7 oz pasta shapes, such as bows or twists
chopped chives

1. Put the pepper strips into the steamer tier.

2. Into a bowl that will fit alongside the peppers, put the cheese. Gradually blend in the stock. Season to taste with salt and pepper. Cover with foil, crimping the edges securely to the sides of the dish. Sit the dish beside the peppers.

3. Pour water in the base of the steamer, sufficient to cover the pasta but not so much that it will boil up into the tier, and add salt. Bring to a rolling boil and stir in the pasta. When the water returns to the boil, stir the pasta, then assemble the steamer.

4. Cover with the lid and steam for about 10 minutes, or for the cooking time given on the pasta packet, until the pasta is just tender, the peppers are soft and the sauce is hot.

5. Drain the pasta thoroughly. Add the peppers. Stir the sauce and add to the mixture. Toss lightly until coated. Serve immediately in warm bowls, sprinkled with chives.

Pasta with Frankfurters and Mustard Sauce

This is simple and delicious. In the sauce, the onion remains slightly crunchy and the mustard is not thoroughly cooked, so remember to use a mild onion (I use red) and adjust the type of mustard to suit your taste.

Serves 2

300g/10½ oz frankfurters
125g packet light soft cheese
150ml/¼ pt vegetable stock
1 tbsp wholegrain mustard
1 small red onion, very thinly sliced into rings and separated
200g/7 oz pasta shapes

1. Arrange the frankfurters in the upper steamer tier.

2. Put the cheese into a bowl that will fit the steamer and gradually blend in the stock. Stir in the mustard and onion. Cover with foil, crimping the edges securely to the sides of the bowl, and stand it in the lower steamer tier.

3. Pour water in the base of the steamer, sufficient to cover the pasta but not so much that it will boil up into the tier, and add salt. Bring to a rolling boil and stir in the pasta. When the water returns to the boil, stir the pasta, then assemble the steamer.

4. Cover with the lid and steam for about 15 minutes.

5. Drain the pasta and tip into a warm serving bowl. Cut the frankfurters into bite-size pieces and add to the pasta. Stir the sauce in the bowl and pour over the pasta. Toss well and serve immediately.

Tagliatelle with Fresh Tomato, Anchovy and Caper Sauce

To ring the changes, you could replace the anchovies with a 200g can of drained and flaked tuna. When choosing capers, I prefer the salted variety (rather than the ones preserved in vinegar) – rinse them well and dry them before using.

Serves 2

8 ripe medium tomatoes
50g can anchovies, drained and chopped
1 generous tbsp capers
3 tbsp finely chopped fresh parsley
salt and freshly ground black pepper
200g/7 oz tagliatelle

1. Make a small slit in the stalk end of each tomato, put them into a bowl and pour over boiling water (from the kettle) to cover. Leave to stand for 5 minutes, after which the skins should peel off easily. Roughly chop the flesh.

2. Mix together the tomatoes, anchovies, capers and parsley. Season with salt and pepper (remembering that the anchovies and capers are quite salty).

3. Line the steamer tier with a large square of foil. Add the tomato mixture. Gather the foil edges together, enclosing the tomatoes, and seal the edges securely.

4. Pour water in the base of the steamer, sufficient to cover the pasta but not so much that it will boil up into the tier, and add salt. Bring to a rolling boil and stir in the pasta. When the water returns to the boil, stir the pasta, then assemble the steamer.

5. Cover with the lid and steam for about 10-12 minutes, or the cooking time given on the tagliatelle packet, until the pasta is just tender.

6. Drain the tagliatelle well. Tear open the foil parcel and pour the sauce over. Toss lightly until coated. Serve immediately in warm bowls.

7
FISH

Salmon and Coriander Pâté

This pâté makes a lovely light lunch, served at room temperature or chilled (when it will be quite firm) with crusty bread or crisp biscuits, or as part of a summer buffet. Sometimes, I rub the dishes with garlic butter, or I put a washed, fresh bay leaf in the bottom of each dish – it gives the pâté extra flavour and looks pretty once it is turned out on to a plate. Ring the changes with the herb too – try using dill (1 tbsp only) or basil in place of the coriander.

Serves 4

About 300g/10½ oz skinless salmon fillet
40g/1½ oz soft butter
2 tbsp sherry
1 medium egg
3 tbsp double cream
2 tsp lemon juice or white wine vinegar
salt and freshly ground black pepper
2 tbsp chopped fresh coriander

1. Butter 4 small dishes or ramekins that will fit in the steamer.

2. Cut the salmon into cubes and put into a food processor. Blend until finely chopped. Add the remaining ingredients and blend until smooth.

3. Spoon the mixture into the dishes and level the surface. Cover each dish with buttered foil, crimping the edges securely to the sides.

4. Put the dishes into the steamer and cover with the lid. Steam for 20 minutes.

5. Leave to cool, then chill until ready to serve. Run a small knife around the edge of the dishes and turn the pâté out on to plates.

Plaice Rolls with Lemon and Spring Onions

Choose plaice fillets that have had black (rather than white) skin removed – they will be thicker. This recipe is also good when made with lemon or Dover sole. Serve with fresh steamed vegetables or a mixed salad.

Serves 4

1 lemon, scrubbed
25g/1 oz butter
85g/3 oz fresh breadcrumbs
3 spring onions, finely chopped
salt and freshly ground black pepper
8 plaice fillets

1.   Finely grate the rind off half the lemon and squeeze 1 tbsp juice from the same half.

2.   Melt the butter and stir in the lemon rind and 1 tbsp juice. Add the breadcrumbs, onions and seasoning and stir lightly until well mixed.

3.   Spread the breadcrumb mixture over the skinned sides of the plaice and roll up each one.

4.   Arrange in the steamer and cover with the lid. Steam for 6-8 minutes until just cooked through.

Salmon with Vegetable Ribbons

Encourage your diners to open their own parcels – to enjoy the wonderful aroma that wafts out. Serve with whole baby potatoes (which could be cooked in the water in the steamer pan).

Serves 4

1 medium courgette
1 small red pepper, halved and seeds removed
2 spring onions
4 skinless salmon fillets, each weighing about 150g/5½ oz
salt and freshly ground black pepper
4 tsp dry white vermouth
butter
4 dill sprigs

1. Using a vegetable peeler, cut the courgette lengthways into long thin ribbons. Cut the pepper into long, thin strips. Half the onions crossways, then cut each piece lengthways into quarters to make thin strips.

2. Arrange one salmon fillet on a piece of baking paper or foil, large enough to enclose it completely. Scatter one quarter of the vegetables on the top. Season with salt and pepper, drizzle over 1 tsp vermouth and top with a knob of butter and a sprig of dill. Close the parcel, leaving plenty of space around the contents and sealing the edges well. Repeat the process with the remaining salmon to make four parcels.

3. Arrange the parcels in one or two steaming tiers, assemble the steamer and cover with the lid. Steam for 6-8 minutes or until the fish is cooked.

Mediterranean Cod Parcels

The tomatoes provide a good quantity of juice that is delicious mopped up with some crusty bread. To reduce the liquid produced, simply remove the seeds from the tomatoes before adding them in step 2. I like to use olives that still have their stones but use pitted ones if you prefer. Also, I like capers that are preserved in salt (rinse them before use) though the varieties in vinegar are good too (drained and rinsed).

Serves 2

2 large ripe tomatoes
2 skinless white fish fillets, such as cod or haddock, each
  weighing about 175g/6 oz
8 black olives
2 tsp capers
salt and freshly ground black pepper
2 tsp extra virgin olive oil

1. Make a small slit in the stalk end of each tomato, put them into a small bowl and pour over boiling water (from the kettle) to cover. Leave to stand for 5 minutes, after which the skins should peel off easily. Chop the flesh into small pieces.

2. Arrange one fish fillet on a piece of baking paper or foil, large enough to enclose it completely. Scatter over half the chopped tomatoes, 4 olives and 1 tsp capers. Season with salt and pepper, then drizzle over 1 tsp oil. Close the parcel, leaving plenty of space around the contents and sealing the edges well. Repeat with the remaining fish to make two parcels.

3. Put the parcels into the steamer and cover with the lid. Steam for 6-8 minutes or until the fish is cooked.

Whole Bass with Oyster Sauce, Ginger and Chilli

This recipe is also ideal for other whole fish, such as salmon, trout, mullet, red snapper or small cod and haddock. Unless steaming is to be completed in a large wok, I usually find it necessary to remove the heads of the fish (and sometimes their tails too) before cooking – so that they fit into the steamer. If you do not have any root ginger sauce, use fresh ginger juice: roughly grate a piece of root ginger (skin and all), then gather it up in one hand and squeeze tightly until ginger juice runs through your fingers. The type (and heat) of the chillies to use is a matter of taste which I leave to you. Do take care when handling chillies to wash your hands well and avoid touching your eyes and other sensitive areas.

Serves 2

2 whole bass, each weighing about 300g/10½ oz, cleaned
2 tbsp oyster sauce
1 tbsp root ginger sauce
2 large spring onions, thinly sliced diagonally
1 garlic clove, cut into fine slivers
1 small red chilli, seeds removed and cut into fine slivers
1 small green chilli, seeds removed and cut into fine slivers

1. Wash and dry the fish inside and out. With a sharp knife, make three or four diagonal slashes down each side of the fish.

2. Mix together the oyster and ginger sauces and brush the mixture over the fish, inside and out.

3. Lay the fish on a sheet of baking paper in the steamer tier.

4. Combine the remaining ingredients and scatter over the fish.

5. Assemble the steamer and cover with the lid. Steam for about 18 minutes until the fish is just cooked through.

Fish on a Bed of Leaves with Parsley Pesto

The lettuce leaves help to collect and retain all the juices and can be served alongside the fish. In spring, I like to replace the lettuce with a thick layer of wild garlic leaves (I am lucky to be able to pick bags of it from the banks of the river Clydach, near my home) which infuse the fish with a delicate garlicky flavour. The pesto can be made as smooth or as coarse as you wish to blend it. This dish is good served with freshly cooked pasta, such as tagliatelle.

Serves 4

25g/1 oz parsley sprigs
1 tbsp chopped chives or spring onion tops
25g/1 oz piece of Parmesan or Pecorino cheese
1 plump garlic clove, sliced
salt and freshly ground black pepper
85ml/3 fl oz olive oil
lettuce leaves
4 fish fillets, such as salmon, cod, or haddock, each weighing about 175g/6 oz
2 tbsp fresh lemon or lime juice
2 spring onions, thinly sliced

1. Make the pesto. Put the herbs, cheese, garlic and seasoning into a food processor and blend until the mixture is coarsely chopped. Add the oil and blend until just combined. Spoon into a small serving dish.

2. Line the steamer basket with lettuce leaves, arranging them so that they reach up the sides a little. Lay the fish on top, skin side down, in a single layer. Season lightly with salt and pepper, then sprinkle over the lemon or lime juice and the onions.

3. Assemble the steamer and cover with the lid. Steam for about 10 minutes or until the fish is just cooked.

4. Serve the fish with its juices, the lettuce (if wished) and the pesto spooned over the top.

Smoked Haddock with Spiced Basmati Rice

When buying smoked haddock, choose the undyed variety if you can. Basmati rice often needs rinsing or soaking in cold water so, before steaming, follow the instructions on the packet.

Serves 4

175g/6 oz basmati rice
4 tsp oil
25g/1 oz sultanas
25g/1 oz shelled unsalted pistachio nuts
1 tbsp curry paste
500g/1 lb 2 oz skinless smoked haddock, bones removed
salt and freshly ground black pepper
4 spring onions, sliced
2-3 tbsp chopped fresh coriander

1. Put the rice into a bowl that will fit into the steamer tier. Stir in the oil, then add the sultanas and nuts. In a measuring jug, blend the curry paste with a little water, then gradually stir in cold water to make up 300ml/½ pt. Stir into the rice.

2. Put the uncovered bowl into the steamer and cover with the lid. Steam for 20 minutes.

3. Arrange the fish, in a single layer if possible, on top of the rice and season with pepper. Scatter the spring onions over the top.

4. Steam for a further 6 minutes or until the fish flakes and the rice is cooked.

5. Carefully turn the fish and rice mixture into a large serving dish. Adjust seasoning to taste, break up the fish roughly and mix together gently.

6. Sprinkle the coriander over the top and serve immediately.

Peppered Salmon with Warm Tomato Salsa

Grind the pepper in a pepper mill or crack it with a pestle and mortar. Salmon steaks (cut across the bone) are ideal for this recipe, though skinned salmon fillets work well too.

Serves 2

freshly ground or cracked black pepper
2 salmon steaks, each weighing about 175g/6 oz
10 cherry tomatoes, halved
1 large or 2 small sun-dried tomatoes in oil, drained and finely chopped
2 spring onions, thinly sliced
2 tsp oil from the sun-dried tomatoes
2 tsp balsamic vinegar
½ tsp caster sugar
8-10 fresh basil leaves

1. Sprinkle pepper over both sides of the salmon steaks, pressing it into the fish. I like quite a bit of pepper, but do add as much or as little as you prefer. Arrange on a sheet of baking paper in a steamer tier.

2. Except for the basil, mix the remaining ingredients together in a bowl that will fit into the steamer, either alongside the salmon or in a second tier. Cover with foil, crimping the edges against the sides of the dish. Place in a steamer tier.

3. Assemble the steamer and cover with the lid. Steam for about 8 minutes or until the fish is just cooked.

4. Roughly tear the basil leaves and gently stir them into the warm tomatoes. Serve the salmon topped with the tomato salsa.

Smoked Haddock with Spinach and Egg

This is probably my husband Huw's favourite weekend lunch. For best results, use undyed smoked haddock and those baby spinach leaves that are meant to be served in salads. Don't be tempted to leave out the freshly grated nutmeg – it makes all the difference to the flavour of the finished dish. I like to garnish it with halved cherry tomatoes.

Serves 2

2 large eggs
2 tbsp double cream
freshly grated nutmeg
2 pieces of smoked haddock fillet, each weighing about 175g/6 oz
225g/8 oz baby spinach leaves

1.   Break the eggs into two, small, buttered dishes or ramekins. Top each one with 1 tbsp cream and sprinkle over some freshly grated nutmeg. Cover with foil, crimping the edges against the sides of the dishes.

2.   If you have a three-tier steamer, put the eggs at the bottom, the fish in the middle and the spinach piled in the top. If one tier only is available, lay the haddock on top of the spinach and squeeze the dishes alongside.

3.   Assemble the steamer and cover with the lid. Steam for about 8 minutes until the eggs are just set and the fish is cooked.

4.   To serve, arrange the haddock on a bed of spinach leaves. Run a knife round the edge of the eggs and turn out on top of the fish.

Wrapped Fish with Spices

This is a useful recipe for any fish that, once cooked, tends to fall apart easily. The leaves hold it together and also seal in the spices that have been rubbed on to the surface of the fish. I mix the spices with a little oil but, if you prefer, rub the dry spice mixture over the fish.

Serves 4

2 tbsp olive oil
1 garlic clove, crushed
2.5cm/1 in piece of fresh root ginger, peeled, finely chopped and crushed
1 tbsp dried oregano
2 tsp ground cumin
1 tsp ground coriander
1 tsp paprika
¼ tsp freshly ground black pepper
good pinch of salt
4 thick skinless fillets of white fish, such as cod, haddock, hake, each weighing about 175g/6 oz
about 150g/5½ oz large spinach leaves, thick stalks removed

1. Mix together the first nine ingredients and rub over all surfaces of the fish.

2. In a large bowl, pour boiling water (from the kettle) over the spinach and leave until just wilted and soft. Drain and rinse under cold water. Lightly pat dry with kitchen paper.

3. On a board or worktop, lay the spinach leaves, overlapping each other, to make four squares, each large enough to enclose a fish fillet completely. Lay one piece of fish on each square and wrap the spinach around it, making sure there are no gaps.

4. Arrange in the steamer and cover with the lid. Steam for about 12 minutes until the fish is cooked through.

Tuna with Thyme and a Mediterranean Topping

The flavour combination of these ingredients reminds me of relaxed holidays in the hot sunshine and long, lazy lunches in the shade of some canopied restaurant. When you first tear open your parcel, you will appreciate just what I mean! Serve them with crusty bread and a crisp green salad.

Serves 2

1 tbsp olive oil
1 tbsp lemon juice
1 garlic clove, crushed
2 tbsp fresh thyme leaves
salt and freshly ground black pepper
2 tuna steaks, each weighing about 175g/6 oz
1 small red onion, thinly sliced into rings
10 cherry tomatoes
6 green olives, sliced into rings

1. Put the oil, lemon juice, garlic, thyme and seasoning into a shallow non-metallic dish, large enough to hold the tuna in a single layer. Add the tuna and turn to coat it well. Cover and leave to stand for about 30 minutes or up to 2 hours, turning it occasionally.

2. Lay each tuna steak on a piece of baking paper or foil, large enough to enclose it completely. Scrape the juices from the dish and drizzle them over the top. Separate the onion slices into rings and arrange them on the tuna. Add the tomatoes and olives. Close the parcel, leaving plenty of space around the contents and sealing the edges well.

3. Arrange in the steamer and cover with the lid. Steam for about 12 minutes until the tuna is just cooked.

Seafood Parcels

This recipe uses white fish, mussels and prawns but you can vary your choice of seafood to suit yourself. Just buy a small amount of several types of fish – such as salmon, monkfish, tuna, clams, oysters and cockles. Serve with fresh bread to mop up the delicious juices.

Serves 2

50g/1¾ oz soft butter
1 small garlic clove, crushed
1 tsp finely chopped fresh parsley
freshly ground black pepper
225g/8 oz raw prawns in their shells, heads and legs removed
225g/8 oz raw mussels in their shells, scrubbed
2 tbsp dry white wine or vermouth
2 tbsp double cream
lemon wedges, to serve

1. With a fork, blend together the butter, garlic, parsley and pepper.

2. Divide the prawns and mussels between two large squares of thick (or double) foil, gathering up the sides. Into each parcel spoon half the wine and half the cream. Top with half the butter mixture. Seal the foil tightly, leaving plenty of room inside for the mussels to open.

3. Put the parcels into one or, preferably, two steamer tiers and cover with the lid. Steam for about 10-15 minutes or until the mussels have opened and the prawns are pink.

4. Serve with the lemon wedges for squeezing over.

Cod with Fresh Tomatoes and Herbs

This dish was inspired by a visit to a Greek island, where fresh sun-ripened tomatoes, garlic and herbs were served up in almost every meal. Use any white fish to suit your taste or your pocket and serve it with new potatoes and a crisp green salad. This recipe can be cooked in individual foil or baking paper parcels too.

Serves 2

225g/8 oz ripe tomatoes
2 tbsp olive oil
1 garlic clove, crushed
½ tsp sugar
2 tbsp finely chopped fresh herbs, such as parsley, thyme or oregano
salt and freshly ground black pepper
2 cod steaks or fillets, each weighing 175-225g/6-8 oz

1.   To skin the tomatoes, use a sharp knife to make a small slit in the skin of each tomato. Put them into a bowl and cover with boiling water (from the kettle). Leave to stand for 5 minutes, after which you can drain them and the skins will slip off easily. Halve the tomatoes, scoop out and discard the seeds and finely chop the flesh.

2.   Combine the chopped tomatoes, oil, garlic, sugar, herbs and a generous quantity of seasoning.

3.   Lay the fish in a lightly oiled shallow dish that will fit in the steamer. Spoon the tomato mixture on top. Cover with foil, crimping the edges securely against the sides of the dish.

4.   Steam for about 30 minutes until the fish flakes.

Haddock and Prawn Mousse

Make a small amount of haddock and prawns into a delicious starter or snack for four. Serve these warm or chilled, garnished with whole prawns, lemon wedges and chopped fresh parsley.

Serves 4 as a starter, 2 as a main course

150g/5½ oz skinless haddock
100ml/3½ fl oz milk
1 bay leaf
1 lemon slice
50g/1¾ oz cooked, peeled prawns, plus 4 in their shells for serving
2 tbsp fresh white breadcrumbs
1 tbsp finely chopped fresh parsley
1 medium egg, separated
dash of hot chilli sauce
salt and freshly ground black pepper
lemon wedges and chopped fresh parsley, to serve

1. Put the haddock into a small frying pan and add the milk, bay leaf and a slice from the lemon half. Cover and cook gently for about 5 minutes or until the fish is cooked.
2. Oil four small 150ml/¼ pt dishes or ramekins. From the remaining lemon, cut four thin slices and place one in the base of each dish.
3. Chop the peeled prawns and put into a bowl. Stir in the breadcrumbs, parsley and egg yolk. Add the cooking juices from the haddock. Flake the haddock, discarding the bay leaf, lemon and any bones. Stir the fish into the prawn mixture. Season to taste with chilli sauce, salt and pepper. Whisk the egg white to stiff peaks and, with a metal spoon, gently fold into the fish.
4. Spoon the mixture into the oiled dishes. Cover with baking paper and then foil, crimping the edges securely to the sides of the dishes.
5. Arrange the dishes in the steamer and cover with the lid. Steam for 30 minutes.
6. Leave to stand for about 5 minutes, before removing the covers, running a flat knife around the edges and carefully turning out on to warm plates. Serve garnished with the whole prawns, lemon wedges and chopped parsley. (To serve cold, leave to cool completely in the dishes and chill overnight before turning out.)

8
POULTRY AND MEAT

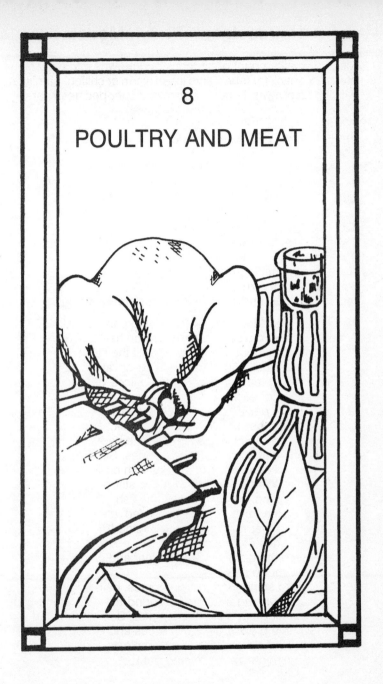

Chicken in a Packet with Tarragon and Cream Sauce

There's lots of sauce, so serve this with crusty bread or rice (steamed above or below the chicken). To serve, simply tear open a foil parcel and allow the contents to slide out on to a warm serving plate.

Serves 2

2 boneless chicken breasts, skin removed
salt and freshly ground black pepper
1½ tbsp chopped fresh tarragon or 1 tsp dried
1 small leek, thinly sliced
1 small carrot, cut into thin matchsticks
4 tsp vermouth or dry white wine
4 tsp double cream

1. Season the chicken breasts lightly with salt and pepper, then put each one on to a piece of foil, large enough to enclose it completely. Sprinkle the tarragon over the chicken. Pile the leek and carrot on top, then spoon over the vermouth and cream. Season the vegetables lightly with salt and pepper.

2. Close the parcels, securing the edges.

3. Put the parcels in the steamer and cover with the lid. Steam for 15-20 minutes until the chicken is cooked through (the juices should run clear when the chicken is pierced with the point of a sharp knife).

Spiced Chicken Breasts

You will need a pestle and mortar, spice mill or an electric coffee grinder to grind the roast spices in this recipe. Don't be put off by the pale, slightly curdled look of the cooked juices – they are deliciously aromatic. I like to serve this with freshly steamed couscous or the Couscous with Pimientos and Black Olives on page 51. Remember to take care when handling chillies to wash your hands well and avoid touching your eyes and other sensitive areas.

Serves 4

2 tsp coriander seeds
1 tsp cumin seeds
1 tsp black peppercorns
4 boneless chicken breasts, skin removed
¼ tsp salt
1 garlic clove, crushed
150ml/¼ pt apple juice
2 tsp sesame oil
salt and freshly ground black pepper
3 spring onions, sliced diagonally
1 small red chilli, seeds removed and cut into very thin rings (optional)

1. In a small frying pan, gently heat the seeds and peppercorns, shaking them occasionally until they begin to brown (they will probably jump about in the pan too). Transfer the mixture to a pestle and mortar, spice mill or cleaned coffee grinder. Grind them to a powder.
2. With a sharp knife, make three or four diagonal cuts into the top surface of each chicken breast.
3. Tip the spices into a shallow ovenproof dish, large enough to hold the chicken in a single layer (make sure it will fit into the steamer). Add the salt, garlic, apple juice and oil and mix well. Slide the chicken breasts into the mixture, turning them until well coated. Cover and refrigerate for about 2 hours, turning the chicken in the marinade occasionally.
4. Season with pepper, then sprinkle the onions and chilli (if using) over the chicken. Cover the dish with foil, crimping the edges against the sides of the dish.
5. Put the dish into the steamer and cover with the lid. Steam for 15-20 minutes or until the juices run clear when the chicken is pierced with the point of a sharp knife.

Fragrant Chicken

If you like moist succulent chicken that is delicately flavoured with spices, onion, lemon and garlic, then this recipe is for you. For the best flavour, I like to use a free range chicken. To cook, the whole chicken sits in the steamer, neck end down – so you will need an electric steamer, a large pan with a deep basket, or a large pan with a steaming stand on which the chicken can sit. Serve it hot or cold with a mixture of fresh salads.

Serves 6

1.6kg/3½ lb chicken
¾ tsp ground coriander
¾ tsp ground cumin
¾ tsp ground cinnamon
½ tsp fresh ground black pepper
¼ tsp ground cloves
1 small onion, quartered
1 lemon, cut into about 8 pieces
3 garlic cloves, peeled and halved

1. Wash and dry the chicken inside and out.

2. Mix together the coriander, cumin, cinnamon, pepper and cloves. Sprinkle about one third of the mixture in the cavity of the chicken, then fill the cavity with the onion, lemon and 2 cloves of garlic.

3. Using your fingers, carefully lift the breast skin, easing it away from the breast as far as your fingers will allow and taking care not to tear it (though it's not the end of the world if you do). Crush the remaining garlic clove and blend it with half of the remaining spice mixture. Spread this between the skin and the breast of the chicken.

4. Rub the remaining spice mixture evenly over the outer surface of the chicken.

5. Sit the chicken in the steamer, cover with the lid and steam for 1¼-1½ hours until the chicken is tender throughout.

Chicken and Tarragon Moulds

Serve these 'terrines' chilled as part of a salad or as a starter to an elegant meal. They look pretty when cut in half and garnished with some baby salad leaves. A salad of thinly sliced tomatoes, sprinkled with oil-and-vinegar dressing, makes an ideal accompaniment.

Makes 4

about 50g/1¾ oz small spinach leaves
1 medium carrot, very thinly sliced
1 medium courgette, thinly sliced
3 boneless chicken breasts, skinned and cut into cubes
1 tbsp chopped fresh tarragon or 1 tsp dried
2 tsp wholegrain mustard
salt and freshly ground black pepper
2 medium egg whites
75ml/2½ fl oz double cream

1. Put the spinach leaves into a bowl and pour over boiling water (from the kettle). Drain immediately (the leaves only need to wilt) and rinse with cold water. Dry gently on kitchen paper. Use the damp leaves to line the base and sides of four dishes or ramekins, each able to hold about 200ml/7 fl oz.

2. Put the carrot slices into a bowl, cover with boiling water and leave to stand. Put the courgette slices into another bowl, cover with boiling water and leave to stand.

3. Put the chicken into a food processor and blend until finely chopped and smooth (alternatively, pass the chicken twice through a mincer). Tip into a bowl and stir in the tarragon and mustard, seasoning generously. Lightly whisk the egg whites until just frothy and stir in to the chicken, a little at a time. Stir in the cream.

4. Spoon enough of the chicken mixture into the dishes to fill them by about one third. Drain and dry the courgette and arrange the slices on top of the chicken, pressing them down lightly. Spoon half the remaining chicken mixture over the top. Drain and dry the carrot and

arrange the slices on top of the chicken, pressing them down lightly. Spoon the remaining chicken over the top and level the surface.

5. Cover with baking paper and then foil, crimping the edges securely to the sides of the dishes.

6. Arrange the dishes in the steamer and cover with the lid. Steam for about 30 minutes until the chicken is firm to the touch and cooked through.

7. Leave to cool covered, then refrigerate for a couple of hours or overnight.

8. To serve, use a flat knife to ease the moulds out of the dishes gently. Cut each one in half vertically to show the layers inside.

Chicken, Bacon and Herb Pudding

Here is an old-fashioned pudding that has always been one of my favourites. For the best flavour and texture, use a mixture of chicken breast and thigh meat. Serve with a green vegetable.

Serves 4

400g/14 oz skinless, boneless chicken
200g/7 oz lean unsmoked gammon
1 medium onion, finely chopped
salt and freshly ground black pepper
1½ tbsp finely chopped fresh parsley or 1½ tsp dried
  herb, such as thyme
175g/6 oz self-raising flour
85g/3 oz shredded suet
150ml/¼ pt chicken or vegetable stock

1. Cut the chicken into bite-size pieces. Remove the rind and any fat from the gammon and cut into bite-size pieces. In a large bowl, mix together the chicken, gammon, onion, seasoning and 1 tbsp parsley (or 1 tsp dried herb).
2. Sift the flour into another large bowl and stir in the suet and ½ tbsp parsley or ½ tsp dried thyme. With a round-blade knife, stir in sufficient water to make a soft dough. Knead lightly until smooth. On a lightly floured surface, roll out the dough into a circle with a diameter of about 32cm/13 in. With a sharp knife, cut off one quarter, roll into a ball and reserve.
3. Lightly butter a 1.2 litre/2 pt pudding basin. Carefully lift the large piece of dough and use it to line the basin, pressing the edges together well. The pastry should overlap the top of the basin slightly.
4. Spoon the chicken mixture into the lined basin, pressing it down carefully and taking care not to split the pastry. Pour in the stock.
5. Roll out the remaining pastry into a circle to form a lid, slightly larger than the top of the basin. Lay on top and seal the edges by pressing them together well.
6. Cover with baking paper and then a large sheet of foil. Gather up the edges, crimping them securely to the sides of the basin.
7. Put into the steamer and cover with the lid. Steam for about 3½ hours, topping up the water as necessary. Serve the pudding straight from the basin.

Chicken and Vegetable Wraps, Mexican Style

If you have eaten and enjoyed Chicken Fajitas, this 'self assembly' meal will resemble a low-fat variation of that dish. It's delicious!

Serves 2

2 tbsp light soy sauce
¼ tsp hot pepper sauce (such as Tabasco) or to taste
2 boneless chicken breasts, skinned
1 small ripe avocado
1 tsp lemon or lime juice
1 tbsp chopped fresh chives
75ml/2½ fl oz soured cream
1 red pepper, seeds removed and cut into strips
8 button mushrooms, preferably the chestnut variety
1 small-to-medium red onion, quartered
4 tortillas
finely shredded lettuce, to serve

1. Put the soy and pepper sauces into a bowl and stir in the chicken. Cover and leave to stand for about 30 minutes (or longer in the refrigerator), stirring occasionally.

2. Halve the avocado and remove the stone. With a teaspoon, scoop the flesh into a bowl. Sprinkle the lemon juice over and mash until smooth. Set aside.

3. In another bowl, stir the chives into the soured cream. Set aside.

4. Arrange the chicken in the bottom steamer tier. In the top tier, put the pepper strips, mushrooms and onion (separated into layers). Wrap the tortillas in foil, sealing the opening well, and lay on top of the vegetables.

5. Assemble the steamer and cover with the lid. Steam for about 15 minutes until the chicken is cooked through, the vegetables are soft and the tortillas are warm.

6. To serve, put two tortillas on each warm serving plate and help yourselves to the toppings – sliced chicken, vegetables, avocado, cream and lettuce – roll up the tortilla and enjoy!

Chicken with Saffron Butter and Pine Nuts

The warm, distinctive flavour of the saffron infuses into the buttery onion mixture to form a sauce. Delicious served with couscous steamed in chicken stock.

Serves 2

50g/1¾ oz butter
pinch of saffron threads
1 small onion, thinly sliced
1 garlic clove, crushed
40g/1½ oz pine nuts
2 boneless chicken breasts, skinned
salt and freshly ground black pepper
4 fresh bay leaves
2 tsp lemon juice

1. Melt the butter gently in a small non-stick frying pan. Add the saffron, onion and garlic and cook over medium heat for 5-10 minutes, stirring occasionally, or until the onion is very soft but not brown. Add the pine nuts, increase the heat slightly beneath the pan and cook for a further 3-5 minutes, stirring occasionally, until the onion and nuts begin to turn golden brown.

2. Put each chicken breast on to a square of baking paper or foil, large enough to enclose it completely. Season, add the bay leaves, then scatter the onion mixture over the top, scraping all the buttery juices from the pan. Sprinkle the lemon juice over. Seal the parcels, securing the edges well.

3. Put the parcels in the steamer and cover with the lid. Steam for about 15 minutes until the chicken is cooked through.

Chicken Wrapped in Parma Ham and Lettuce

The ham and lettuce wraps add a delicate flavour to the chicken and help to keep it succulent too. I like to serve this with Baby Vegetables with Lime and Pesto (page 39).

Serves 2

2 boneless chicken breasts, skinned
salt and freshly ground black pepper
2 slices of Parma ham
2 large lettuce leaves, such as cos, each large enough to enclose a chicken breast completely

1. Season the chicken breasts with salt and pepper. Wrap a slice of ham around each one.

2. Put the lettuce leaves into a shallow dish and pour over boiling water (from the kettle). As soon as the leaves have wilted and are pliable, drain off the water and pat them dry with kitchen towel. Wrap one leaf around each piece of chicken to enclose it completely.

3. Put the chicken in the steamer and cover with the lid. Steam for about 15 minutes until the chicken is cooked through (the juices should run clear when pierced with a skewer).

Old-Fashioned Steak Pudding

To my mind, there is nothing that can compete with the rich flavour of a meat pudding cooked in the steamer. The meat is meltingly soft and sits in a golden, lemony pastry crust – real winter food. Serve it piping hot with a green vegetable to accompany it.

Serves 4-6

750g/1 lb 10 oz lean stewing steak, cut into bite-size cubes
1 medium onion, finely chopped
2 tbsp finely chopped fresh herbs, such as parsley, or 2
   tsp dried mixed herbs
1½ tbsp flour
salt and freshly ground black pepper
175g/6 oz self-raising flour
85g/3 oz shredded suet
finely grated rind of 1 lemon
about 100ml/3½ fl oz beef stock or water

1. Put the steak, onion and herbs into a large bowl. Season the 1½ tbsp flour with salt and pepper and add to the bowl. Toss the steak mixture well until evenly coated with the seasoned flour.

2. Sift the self-raising flour into another large bowl and stir in the suet and lemon rind. With a round-bladed knife, stir in sufficient water to make a soft dough. Knead lightly until smooth. On a lightly floured surface, roll out the dough into a circle with a diameter of about 32cm/13 in. With a sharp knife, cut off one quarter, roll into a ball and reserve.

3. Lightly butter a 1.2 litre/2 pt pudding basin. Carefully lift the large piece of dough and use it to line the basin, pressing the edges together well. The pastry should overlap the top of the basin slightly.

4. Spoon the steak mixture into the lined basin, pressing it down carefully, taking care not to split the pastry. Pour in sufficient stock or water to reach about three-quarters of the way up the filling.

5. Roll out the remaining pastry into a circle to form a lid, slightly larger than the top of the basin. Lay on top and seal the edges by pressing them together well.

6. Cover with baking paper and then a large piece of foil. Gather up the edges, crimping them securely to the sides of the basin.

7. Put into the steamer and cover with the lid. Steam for about 4½ hours, topping up the water when necessary. Serve the hot pudding straight from the basin.

Steak and Mushroom Pudding

Cover 20g/¾ oz dried porcini mushrooms with boiling water and leave to soak for 30 minutes. Drain and finely chop the mushrooms, straining and saving the liquid. Make the strained mushroom liquid up to about 100ml/3½ fl oz with beef stock or water. Now make Old-Fashioned Steak Pudding, adding the chopped mushrooms in step 1.

Steak and Kidney Pudding

Make Old-Fashioned Steak Pudding, replacing 175g/6 oz steak with trimmed and chopped kidney.

Steak and Ale Pudding

Make Old-Fashioned Steak Pudding, replacing the beef stock or water with brown ale. Stir 1-2 tbsp wholegrain mustard into the ale before adding it to the pudding.

Pork Ribs, Oriental Style

Pork ribs are steamed until the meat almost falls from the bone. Though it is not essential to brown the pork in step 2, I think the flavour and appearance benefit from it. The root ginger sauce can be replaced with some finely grated root ginger if preferred. It's good served with steamed rice (put in the top tier and added towards the end of the cooking time.

Serves 2-3

3 tsp soy sauce
1 tbsp sesame oil
1 tbsp rice or white wine vinegar
1 generous tbsp oyster sauce
1 tbsp root ginger sauce
1 tbsp caster sugar
900g/2 lb meaty pork spare ribs
2 level tsp cornflour

1. In a shallow non-metallic dish, large enough to hold the pork ribs in a single layer, mix together the first six ingredients. Add the ribs, turning to coat them well. Cover and leave to marinate for up to 2 hours, or refrigerated for longer or overnight, turning them occasionally.

2. Lift the ribs out and reserve the marinade. In a large non-stick frying pan, brown the meat quickly on all sides.

3. Arrange the ribs on a sheet of baking paper in the steamer and cover with the lid. Steam for 1-1½ hours until the pork is tender and is easily pulled away from the bone (remember to top up the boiling water when necessary).

4. Tip the reserved marinade into a small saucepan, whisk in the cornflour and heat, stirring continuously, until the sauce comes to the boil and thickens (alternatively cook in the microwave on full power for about 3 minutes, stirring occasionally, or until the sauce comes to the boil and thickens).

5. Serve the ribs with the sauce spooned over them.

Wrapped Pork with Redcurrant Sauce and Soured Cream

The flavours in this dish are reminiscent of those Danish meatballs called Frikadeller.

Serves 4

8 large cabbage leaves
500g/1 lb 2 oz ground pork
1 level tbsp plain flour
1 bunch of spring onions
salt and freshly ground black pepper
freshly grated nutmeg
1 medium egg, lightly beaten
2 tbsp redcurrant jelly
1 tbsp Worcestershire sauce
4 tbsp soured cream

1. Steam the cabbage leaves for about 10 minutes until wilted and pliable.

2. Meanwhile, put the pork and flour into a large bowl. Finely chop the spring onions, reserving some of the green tops for garnishing, and add to the pork. Season the mixture generously with salt and pepper and add a good grating of nutmeg. Mix well, then stir in the egg.

3. Dry the wilted cabbage leaves by patting them lightly with kitchen paper. Divide the pork mixture between the leaves, placing a mound in the centre of each and rolling up to enclose the meat completely. Lay the parcels in the steamer tier (you may need two).

4. Spoon the redcurrant jelly into a small dish and stir in the Worcestershire sauce. Cover with foil, crimping the edges securely to the sides of the dish. Place in the steamer alongside the pork parcels.

5. Cover with the lid and steam for about 30 minutes or until the parcels are firm to the touch and cooked through.

6. To serve, stir the redcurrant sauce and spoon a little on to a serving plate. Arrange the pork parcels in the sauce, drizzle the soured cream over and scatter the reserved spring onions over the top.

Pork and Pineapple with Coconut and Coriander Sauce

In this dish, discs of pork fillet are served on a slice of pineapple with coconut and coriander sauce spooned over the top. Ideal accompaniments would be freshly cooked noodles, sprinkled with a little sesame oil, and steamed mange tout (add them to the top layer of the steamer for the final 5-10 minutes).

Serves 4

2 tbsp soy sauce
¼ tsp Chinese five spice seasoning
1 tsp clear honey
salt and freshly ground black pepper
550g/1¼ lb pork fillet, cut into 1cm/½ in thick slices
227g can pineapple slices in fruit juice (4 slices)
50g/1¾ oz creamed coconut, finely chopped or grated
1 tsp finely chopped root ginger
1 small garlic clove, crushed (optional)
3 tbsp chopped fresh coriander

1. Put the soy sauce, seasoning and honey into a shallow dish, large enough to take the pork in a single layer. Season with black pepper. Add the pork, turning to coat it well. Cover and leave to marinate for about 2 hours or refrigerated overnight.
2. Put the juice from the pineapple into a bowl and add the coconut, ginger and garlic.
3. Line the bottom steamer tier with baking paper. Lift the pork, reserving the marinade, and arrange the slices in an even layer on the paper.
4. Stir the reserved marinade into the coconut mixture. Season with salt and pepper. Cover the bowl with foil, crimping the edges securely to the sides. Sit the bowl in the second tier together with the pineapple slices (leave them in a stack).
5. Assemble the steamer and cover with the lid. Steam for about 15 minutes until the pork is cooked.
6. To serve, arrange the pork slices on top of the pineapple. Stir the sauce until smooth, then add the coriander. Spoon the sauce over the pork and pineapple.

Pork in Foil – Greek Style

This recipe is based on Stifado, a dish that my husband, Huw, enjoyed in Crete. There, it was cooked in the oven. Since then I have cooked it successfully on the barbecue and now in the steamer. The special background flavour comes from the allspice – if you don't have any to hand, use ground cloves instead.

Serves 2

1 tbsp olive oil, plus extra for brushing
1 small red onion, thinly sliced
300g/10½ oz pork tenderloin, cut diagonally into 1 cm/
   ½ in thick slices
salt and freshly ground black pepper
1 garlic clove, finely chopped
2 medium tomatoes, sliced
2 pinches of ground allspice
4 generous sprigs of thyme
2 tsp red wine vinegar

1. Lightly brush two large squares of foil with oil. On each piece, lay half the onion and half the pork. Season with salt and pepper, scatter the garlic over and add the tomato slices. Sprinkle with allspice, add the thyme sprigs and drizzle over the oil and vinegar.

2. Seal the parcels, securing the edges well. Arrange them in the steamer and cover with the lid.

3. Steam for about 30 minutes until cooked through.

Chinese Steamed Pork Dumplings

Chinese dumplings are ideal for steaming – just witness the variety of ready-made dumplings on offer in the freezers of Chinese supermarkets. Here is a quick recipe for making your own tasty morsels. Serve them hot and remember that dumplings reheat well in the steamer too.

Makes 16

250g/9 oz plain flour
2 level tsp baking powder
250g/9 oz ground pork
2 tbsp soy sauce
1 tbsp sesame oil
1 tbsp dry sherry
1 tsp sugar
1 tsp finely grated fresh root ginger
1 level tsp cornflour
½ tsp salt

1. Sift the flour and baking powder into a bowl and mix in sufficient water to make a pliable dough (about 125ml/ 4 fl oz). Knead well until smooth. Cover the bowl with clear film and leave in a warm place to rest for about 1 hour.

2. Meanwhile mix the pork with the remaining ingredients.

3. On a lightly floured surface, knead the dough until smooth and divide it into 16 balls. Roll one piece into a circle with a diameter of about 7.5cm/3 in. Place a spoonful of the pork mixture in the centre of the pastry, then gather it up and around the filling so that it meets at the top. Pinch the dough tightly to seal it. Repeat with the remaining pastry and filling.

4. Arrange the dumplings in a single layer on baking paper in the steamer. Cover with the lid and steam for 20 minutes.

Lamb with Rosemary and Garlic

Here, a half shoulder of lamb is steamed until the fat drains away and the meat is so meltingly tender that it almost cuts with a fork. I brown the joint in a pan before steaming but you could just as easily finish the lamb in a hot oven after steaming if you wish. Serve it sliced with freshly steamed vegetables and the pan juices (see below) or shredded in hot crusty rolls or warm tortillas with a salad garnish.

Serves 4

about 1-1.2kg/2¼-2¾ lb half shoulder of lamb (boneless if possible)
4 garlic cloves, cut into slivers
fresh rosemary sprigs
salt and freshly ground black pepper
1 lemon
1 tbsp olive oil

1. With the tip of a sharp knife, make several small, deep cuts into the surface of the lamb. Into each cut, push a sliver of garlic and a piece of rosemary. Tuck some in the folds of the meat too. Season the lamb all over with salt and pepper.

2. Squeeze the juice from the lemon, reserving the skins. Sprinkle half the lemon juice over the lamb.

3. Heat the oil in a large non-stick frying pan and quickly brown the lamb well on all sides, sprinkling the remaining lemon juice over as you cook.

4. Lift the lamb into the steamer and drizzle the pan juices over it. Lay the reserved lemon skins on top (they will impart their flavour to the lamb).

5. Cover with the lid and steam for about 1-1¼ hours until the lamb is tender and most of the fat has melted away. Discard the lemon skins before serving.

6. Once the lamb is cooked, you may want to save the delicious pan juices. To do this, skim the fat from the surface with a metal spoon, then boil the remaining juices vigorously until they are reduced, adjusting the seasoning to taste. Serve the lamb, sliced, with the juices poured over.

Lamb with Leeks, Honey and Lemon

I just love this combination of flavours and the pool of sweet juices that collect around the lamb. Don't be tempted to omit the parsley and lemon topping – it makes all the difference.

Serves 2

1 garlic clove, crushed
1 tbsp clear honey
finely grated rind and juice of ½ a lemon
salt and freshly ground black pepper
350g/12 oz lean lamb neck fillet, cut into 1cm/½ in slices
2 small leeks, sliced
2 tbsp finely chopped fresh parsley

1. Put the garlic and honey into a bowl. Blend in the lemon juice and seasoning. Add the lamb slices and toss until coated. Cover and leave to stand for about 30 minutes (or up to 2 hours).

2. Line the bottom steamer tier with baking paper and arrange the lamb in an even layer on top.

3. Put the leeks into the second tier.

4. Assemble the steamer and cover with the lid. Steam for about 15 minutes until the lamb is cooked.

5. Meanwhile, mix together the lemon rind and parsley.

6. To serve, pile the leeks on to warm serving plates and arrange the lamb on top. Spoon over the juices that have collected on the paper and sprinkle the lemon and parsley over the top.

Lamb and Apricot Skewers

Steamed couscous is a natural accompaniment to these kebabs with their flavour that reminds me of North African dishes. They are also good served in warmed and split pitta bread with some finely shredded lettuce.

Serves 2

1 tbsp olive oil
1 garlic clove, crushed
2 tsp clear honey
½ tsp ground cinnamon
¼ tsp ground ginger
¼ tsp ground turmeric
salt and freshly ground black pepper
350g/12 oz lean lamb fillet, thickly sliced
8 ready-to eat dried apricots
chopped fresh parsley
1 tbsp toasted sesame seeds

1. Put the first seven ingredients into a shallow dish and mix well. Add the lamb and stir until well coated. Cover and leave to marinate for at least 1 hour or preferably longer (in the fridge).

2. Thread the lamb and apricots on to four small skewers (wood or metal) that will fit into the steamer, leaving a very small gap between each piece.

3. Arrange the skewers in the steamer tier, overlapping if necessary and leaving room around each one for steam to circulate.

4. Cover with the lid and steam for about 15 minutes until the lamb is cooked.

5. Serve sprinkled with the parsley and toasted sesame seeds.

Smooth Liver Pâté

A deliciously savoury snack or starter, this pâté can be served with crisp toast or biscuits or fresh crusty bread.

Serves 4-6

4 back bacon rashers
350g/12 oz lamb's liver
115g/4 oz chicken livers
4 spring onions, chopped
1 garlic clove, crushed
1 small egg, lightly beaten
1 tsp dried mixed herbs
¼ tsp freshly grated nutmeg
2 tbsp double cream
2 tsp brandy
salt and freshly ground black pepper

1. Choose a 700ml/1¼ pt oval or rectangular dish that fits into the steamer. Line the dish with the bacon, allowing any extra to hang over the sides.

2. Cut the lamb's liver into small pieces and put these and the chicken livers into the food processor and purée until finely chopped (alternatively, put them through a mincer). Add the onions, garlic, egg, herbs, nutmeg, cream, brandy and seasoning and blend until well mixed. Spoon the mixture into the lined dish, folding any extra bacon over the top. Cover with foil, crimping the edges securely against the sides of the dish.

3. Steam for about 1¼ hours until the top feels firm to the touch.

4. Leave to cool, then chill overnight.

5. Turn the pâté out of the dish just before serving.

9
DESSERTS

Marmalade Sponge Pudding

Here is an old-fashioned favourite with some variations. Serve them with plenty of custard, preferably flavoured with vanilla extract.

Serves 4-6

3 tbsp marmalade
100g/3¾ oz soft butter
100g/3¾ oz caster sugar
2 medium eggs, lightly beaten
few drops of vanilla essence
175g/6 oz self-raising flour, sifted
2-3 tbsp milk

1. Butter a 1.2 litre/2 pt pudding basin and spoon the marmalade into the bottom.

2. In a large mixing bowl, beat the butter and sugar together until light and fluffy. Gradually beat in the eggs and vanilla essence then, using a metal spoon, fold in the sifted flour and sufficient milk to make a soft, dropping consistency.

3. Spoon the mixture on top of the marmalade and level the top.

4. Cover with baking paper and then a large piece of foil. Gather up the sides, crimping the edges securely to the sides of the basin.

5. Put into the steamer and cover with the lid. Steam for about 1½ hours, topping up the boiling water as necessary.

6. Leave the cooked pudding to stand for 5 minutes before turning out on to a warm serving plate.

Jam Sponge Pudding

Make Marmalade Sponge Pudding, replacing the marmalade with jam of your choice.

Syrup Sponge Pudding

Make Marmalade Sponge Pudding, replacing the marmalade with golden syrup.

Mincemeat Sponge Pudding

Make Marmalade Sponge Pudding, replacing the marmalade with good-quality mincemeat.

Orange or Lemon Sponge Pudding

Make Marmalade Sponge Pudding, replacing the marmalade with orange or lemon curd and adding the finely grated rind of 1 lemon or orange to the butter-and-sugar mixture in step 2.

Chocolate Pudding

Make Marmalade Sponge Pudding, omitting the marmalade. Blend 4 tbsp cocoa powder with 1 tbsp hot water and stir into the beaten butter and sugar in step 2.

Fruit Sponge Pudding

Make Marmalade Sponge Pudding, replacing the marmalade with fresh, cooked or drained canned fruit.

Mixed Fruit Compote

This is delicious served hot, warm or chilled with cream, custard or thick yogurt. In winter, add some spices, such as a cinnamon stick or a few cloves or star anise. I like to serve the compote, chilled, for breakfast too.

Serves 6

175g/6 oz ready-to-eat dried apricots
175g/6 oz ready-to-eat dried prunes
175g/6 oz ready-to-eat dried figs
25g/1 oz raisins
40g/1½ oz caster sugar
2 fruit teabags, such as blackcurrant

1. Put all the ingredients into a dish and pour over 600ml/ 1 pt boiling water. Cover with foil, crimping the edges securely to the sides of the dish.

2. Put the dish in the steamer and cover with the lid. Steam for 1-1½ hours until the fruit is tender, stirring half way and topping up the boiling water as necessary.

3. Remove the teabags before serving.

Apple and Fig Pudding

This old-fashioned pudding has the most wonderfully rich and fragrant filling. I have to admit that its dull brown appearance leaves much to be desired but the flavour more than makes up for it.

Serves 6

175g/6 oz self-raising flour
85g/3 oz shredded suet
Bramley apples, peeled, cored and sliced – about 350g/ 12 oz prepared weight
150g/5½ oz ready-to-eat dried figs, stalks removed and quartered lengthways
100g/3½ oz soft brown muscovado sugar
1 tbsp lemon juice

1. Sift the flour into a bowl and stir in the suet. With a round-bladed knife, stir in sufficient water to make a soft dough (about 150ml/¼ pt). Knead lightly until smooth.

2. On a lightly floured surface, roll out the dough into a circle with a diameter of about 32cm/13 in. With a sharp knife, cut off one quarter, roll up and reserve.

3. Lightly butter a 1.2 litre/2 pt pudding basin. Carefully lift the large piece of dough and use it to line the basin, pressing the edges together well. The pastry should overlap the top of the basin slightly.

4. Into a large bowl, put the apple, figs, sugar and lemon juice. Stir until well mixed. Spoon the mixture evenly into the lined basin, pressing down gently (take care not to tear the pastry).

5. Roll out the remaining pastry into a circle to form a lid, slightly larger than the top of the basin. Lay on top and seal the edges by pressing them together well. Cover with baking paper and then with a large piece of foil. Gather the edges together, crimping them securely against the sides of the basin.

6. Put in the steamer and cover with the lid. Steam for about 2½ hours, topping up the boiling water as necessary.

7. Serve the pudding straight from the basin.

Spotted Dick

Traditionally Spotted Dick would have been made with shredded suet, shaped into a roll about 15cm/6 in long, wrapped loosely in a pudding cloth and boiled. I like it made with butter and steamed in a pudding bowl. (If you wish, you can of course replace the butter with shredded suet.) Serve it hot with plenty of custard flavoured with vanilla extract.

Serves 6

75g/2¾ oz butter
100g/3½ oz fresh breadcrumbs
75g/2¾ oz self-raising flour
50g/1¾ oz caster sugar (I use golden)
140g/5 oz currants
finely grated rind of 1 lemon
about 6 tbsp milk

1. Lightly butter a 1.2 litre/2 pt pudding bowl. Put the block of butter in the freezer for about 20 minutes.

2. Put the breadcrumbs into a mixing bowl, sift in the flour and stir in the sugar, currants and lemon rind. Quickly grate the frozen butter into the bowl, then stir in sufficient milk to make a slightly sticky dough.

3. Spoon the mixture into the prepared bowl and level the surface. Cover with baking paper and then with a large piece of foil. Gather the edges together, crimping them securely against the sides of the basin.

4. Put into the steamer and cover with the lid. Steam for about 1¾ hours, topping up the boiling water as necessary.

5. Turn the pudding out on to a warmed plate and serve immediately.

Christmas Pudding

For the best flavour, make the pudding one or two months before you need it, then let it mature in a cool, dark place. Serve it with a sweet white sauce or brandy butter.

Serves 8-10

50g/1¾ oz plain flour
1 tsp ground mixed spice
1 tsp ground nutmeg
100g/3½ oz fresh breadcrumbs
125g/4½ oz shredded suet
100g/3½ oz soft dark brown sugar
400g/14 oz mixed dried fruit
50g/1¾ oz blanched almonds, roughly chopped
1 small carrot, finely grated
finely grated rind of 1 small orange
2 medium eggs, beaten
2 tbsp brandy or dry sherry
1 tsp almond essence
75ml/2½ fl oz milk

1. Into a large mixing bowl, sift the flour, spice and nutmeg. Mix in the breadcrumbs, suet, sugar, fruit, nuts, carrot and orange rind. Add the eggs, brandy, essence and milk. Mix well.

2. Butter a 1.2 litre/2 pt pudding basin. Spoon the mixture into the prepared basin and level the top. Cover with baking paper and then with a large piece of foil. Gather the edges together, crimping them securely against the sides of the basin.

3. Put into the steamer and cover with the lid. Steam for about 6 hours, topping up the boiling water when necessary.

4. Lift the pudding out of the steamer and leave to stand until cold.

5. Wrap securely with foil and store in a cool place until needed.

To reheat:
Steam the pudding for about 2 hours before turning out on to a warmed serving dish.

Clootie Dumpling

This Scottish dessert, a dumpling traditionally boiled in a cloth, is served at Hogmanay or New Year. Serve it with a custard or fruit sauce. Any leftovers can be served cold, sliced and sprinkled with caster sugar or lightly fried in butter.

Serves 6

75g/2¾ oz self-raising flour
1 tsp baking powder
1 tsp ground cinnamon
1 tsp ground nutmeg
75g/2¾ oz fresh white breadcrumbs
75g/2¾ oz caster sugar
75g/2¾ oz shredded suet
175g/6 oz mixed dried fruit
1 crisp eating apple, such as Cox's, peeled and grated
1 small carrot, finely grated
1 tbsp black treacle
1 medium egg, lightly beaten
finely grated rind of 1 orange
about 150ml/¼ pt milk

1. Into a large mixing bowl, sift the flour, baking powder and spices. Stir in the remaining ingredients and mix well, adding sufficient milk to make a soft (but quite stiff) consistency. Spoon the mixture into a buttered 1.2 litre/ 2 pt pudding basin.

2. Cover with baking paper and then with a large piece of foil. Gather the edges together, crimping them securely against the sides of the basin.

3. Put into the steamer and cover with the lid. Steam for 2-2½ hours until the pudding is well risen and firm to the touch, topping up the boiling water as necessary.

4. Lift the pudding out of the steamer and carefully turn out on to a warm serving plate.

Ginger and Almond Pudding

This is a lovely, light, slightly sticky pudding. Serve it with custard or Greek yogurt.

Serves 4-6

85g/3 oz butter, softened
85g/3 oz caster sugar
85g/3 oz self-raising flour
½ level tsp baking powder
25g/1 oz ground almonds
2 medium eggs, lightly beaten
4 pieces of stem ginger in syrup, drained and finely chopped
1 tbsp syrup from the ginger

1. Butter a 1.2 litre/2 pt pudding bowl and put a small circle of baking paper in the bottom.

2. Put the softened butter and the caster sugar into a large mixing bowl. Sift over the flour and baking powder. Add the remaining ingredients and beat well until smooth.

3. Spoon the mixture into the prepared bowl and level the surface. Cover with baking paper and then with a large piece of foil. Gather the edges together, crimping them securely against the sides of the basin.

4. Put into the steamer and cover with the lid. Steam for 1¼ hours, topping up the boiling water as necessary.

5. To serve, turn the pudding out on to a warm plate and remove the baking paper.

Egg Custard

Cook this in one dish or in individual cups or ramekins. Serve it hot, cool or chilled, just as it is or with fresh fruit, such as strawberries or raspberries, or with steamed fruit.

Serves 4-6

3 medium eggs
25g/1 oz caster sugar
1 tsp vanilla extract
600ml/1 pt single cream or full-cream milk
freshly grated nutmeg

1. Lightly butter a 20 cm/ 8 in soufflé dish or 4-6 cups or ramekins.

2. Beat the eggs with the sugar and vanilla extract. Gradually beat in the cream or milk. Strain the mixture into the prepared dish(es). Sprinkle some freshly grated nutmeg over the top. Cover with foil, crimping the edges securely to the sides of the dish(es).

3. Put into the steamer and cover with the lid. Steam the large pudding for about 20 minutes (the custard should be still slightly wobbly at its centre) or the small ones for about 10 minutes.

4. Remove from the steamer and leave to stand, covered, for 10-15 minutes before serving.

Coconut Rice Pudding

Rice pudding flavoured with coconut cream is a favourite in our family. Serve it with slices of fresh or canned mango. To make a standard rice pud, simply replace the coconut cream with milk or cream.

Serves 4

50g/1¾ oz pudding or round-grain rice
25g/1 oz caster sugar
400ml/14 fl oz full-cream milk
200ml carton coconut cream
½ tsp vanilla extract
20g/¾ oz butter
freshly grated nutmeg

1. Butter a 20cm/8 in soufflé dish. Spoon the rice and sugar over the base of the dish. Stir together the milk, coconut cream and vanilla extract and pour over the rice. Cut the butter into small pieces and dot over the top. Sprinkle some freshly grated nutmeg over the surface. Cover with foil, crimping the edges securely against the sides of the dish.

2. Put into the steamer and cover with the lid. Steam for about 2 hours or until the rice is tender and the pudding has thickened, stirring half way. Top up the boiling water as necessary.

Sussex Pond Pudding

A whole lemon is cooked with butter and brown sugar and surrounded by pastry. When the cooked pudding is cut open, the buttery juices make a pond on the plate. Sometimes, I add some raisins, pushing them into the butter and sugar in step 4. Make sure everyone is served with a piece of the lemon and top it with whipped cream or thick yogurt.

Serves 4-6

225g/8 oz self-raising flour
100g/3¾ oz shredded suet
150g/5½ oz butter, cut into small cubes
150g/5½ oz light, soft brown sugar
1 large unwaxed lemon, well washed

1. Sift the flour into a bowl and stir in the suet. With a round-bladed knife, stir in sufficient water to make a soft dough (about 150ml/½ pt). Knead lightly until smooth.

2. On a lightly floured surface, roll out the dough into a circle with a diameter of about 32cm/13 in. With a sharp knife, cut off one quarter, roll up and reserve.

3. Butter a 1.2 litre/2 pt pudding basin. Carefully lift the large piece of dough and use it to line the basin, pressing the edges together well. The pastry should overlap the top of the basin slightly.

4. Put half the butter and half the sugar into the lined basin. With a thin skewer, prick the lemon all over. Gently press the lemon into the centre of the butter mixture in the basin. Spoon the remaining butter and sugar around the lemon.

5. Roll out the remaining pastry quarter into a circle to form a lid, slightly larger than the top of the basin. Lay on top and seal the edges by pressing them together well. Cover with baking paper and then with a large piece of foil. Gather up the edges, crimping them securely against the sides of the basin.

6. Put into the steamer and cover with the lid. Steam for about 3 hours, topping up the boiling water as necessary.

Passion Pudding with Lemon Syrup Sauce

This moist pudding is based on the cake of the same name. If you are feeling really indulgent, top each portion of pudding and sauce with a spoonful of light cream cheese.

Serves 4-6

100g/3½ oz soft butter
100g/3½ oz light muscovado sugar
2 medium eggs, lightly beaten
100g/3½ oz finely grated carrot
finely grated rind and juice of 1 lemon
100g/3½ oz self-raising flour
¼ tsp baking powder
40g/1½ oz walnuts or pecans, finely chopped
25g/1 oz sultanas or raisins
4 tbsp golden syrup

1. Lightly butter an 850ml/1½ pt pudding bowl and put a small disc of baking paper in the bottom.

2. Put the butter and sugar into a bowl and beat until soft and creamy. Beat in the eggs, a little at a time. Beat in the carrot and lemon rind. Sift the flour and baking powder over the top and, with a metal spoon, fold in. Gently fold in the nuts and fruit.

3. Spoon the mixture into the prepared bowl and level the surface. Cover with baking paper and then a large piece of foil. Gather up the edges, crimping them securely against the sides of the bowl.

4. Put into the steamer and cover with the lid. Steam for 2 hours, topping up the boiling water as necessary.

5. Just before serving, put the lemon juice and syrup into a small pan and heat gently until hot and just bubbling. Alternatively, put the juice and syrup into a bowl and heat in the microwave on full power for about ½ minute or until just bubbling.

6. Serve the pudding with the sauce.

Pecan and Maple Syrup Pudding

Pecan nuts and maple syrup make a heavenly partnership! Use real maple syrup if you can, not the 'flavoured' variety of syrup. Serve each portion topped with a spoonful of Greek yogurt or crème fraîche.

Serves 6

3 tbsp maple syrup
50g/1¾ oz pecan halves
115g/4 oz soft butter
115g/4 oz golden caster sugar
2 medium eggs, lightly beaten
1 tbsp milk
115g/4 oz self-raising flour
1 tsp baking powder

1. Lightly butter a 1.2 litre/2 pt pudding basin and put a small disc of baking paper in the bottom.

2. Spoon the maple syrup into the basin. Arrange half the pecan halves in the syrup and finely chop the rest.

3. Put the butter, sugar, eggs and milk into a mixing bowl and sift over the flour and baking powder. Beat well until smooth, then stir in the chopped nuts. Spoon the mixture into the basin and level the surface.

4. Cover with baking paper and then with a large piece of foil. Gather up the edges, crimping them securely against the sides of the basin.

5. Put into the steamer and cover with the lid. Steam for 2 hours, topping up the boiling water as necessary.

Honeyed Banana and Orange Parcels

This recipe is easy to multiply, so make as many parcels as you need or will fit into the steamer. Serve the parcels just as they are so that each diner opens his or her own. Serve topped with some toasted flaked almonds and/or whipped cream or a scoop of vanilla ice cream.

Serves 2

1 large orange
2 bananas
¼ tsp ground ginger
2 tbsp clear honey
2 tsp dark rum (optional)
15g/½ oz butter (optional)

1. Using a sharp knife, remove the peel (both the rind and the white zest) from the orange and reserve. Slice the orange into rings and arrange on two squares of foil, large enough to enclose the fruit completely. Peel the bananas, slice thickly and lay on top of the orange.

2. Into a small bowl, squeeze the orange juice from the peel. Whisk in the ginger and then the honey and rum (if using). Spoon the mixture over the fruit and top each pile with half the butter (if using).

3. Close the parcels, sealing the foil edges well.

4. Put into the steamer and cover with the lid. Steam for 15 minutes.

Banana Crème Brulée

Most people enjoy this creamy dessert with its crunchy topping. My family loves the additional flavour of the banana as well as the vanilla extract.

Serves 4

4 egg yolks
½ tsp vanilla extract
35g/1¼ oz caster sugar
300ml/½ pt double cream
100ml/3½ fl oz milk
1 banana
demerara sugar

1. Lightly whisk together the egg yolks, vanilla extract and caster sugar.

2. In a pan on the hob or in the microwave, gently heat the cream and milk until hot but not boiling. Pour on to the egg mixture, whisking continuously.

3. Peel and thinly slice the banana and arrange in the base of four small flameproof dishes or ramekins. Strain the cream mixture over the top. Cover with foil, crimping the edges securely to the sides of the dishes.

4. Steam for about 10 minutes or until the custards are only just set (they should still wobble slightly at the centre).

5. Leave to cool, then chill for 1-2 hours.

6. About one hour before serving, sprinkle an even layer of demerara sugar over the top of each custard. Put the dishes under a very hot (preheated) grill for a few minutes until the sugar liquefies, bubbles and turns golden to dark brown. Chill until the sugar topping is cold and crisp.

Warm Berry 'Trifles'

A hot 'trifle' in a foil parcel? Try it and see just how good it is! Instead of amaretti biscuits, you could use sponge fingers or trifle sponges.

Serves 4

**450g/1 lb mixed fresh berries, such as strawberries, rasp-
   berries, cherries, blackberries and blueberries**
4 tsp caster sugar
1 tsp finely chopped fresh mint
4 tsp apple or orange juice
4 tsp fruit liqueur, such as blackcurrant (cassis)
12 amaretti biscuits
whipped cream, crème fraîche or thick yogurt

1. Put the fruit into a bowl and sprinkle the sugar and mint over. Add the juice and liqueur and stir gently until well mixed.

2. Divide the mixture between four squares of foil, each large enough to enclose the fruit completely. Top each pile of fruit with 3 amaretti biscuits.

3. Close the parcels, sealing the foil edges well.

4. Arrange in the steamer and cover with the lid. Steam for 10 minutes.

5. To serve, place the parcels on individual serving plates. Each person opens his or her own 'trifle' and tops it with whipped cream, crème fraîche or thick yogurt.

Brown Bananas with Butterscotch Sauce

Cooking bananas in their skins works in the steamer as well as in the oven and on the barbecue (when their skins turn black). If you need to double the quantities, I suggest that you put the bowl of sauce in the bottom tier of the steamer and the bananas above it. Sometimes, I like to replace the golden syrup with maple syrup.

Serves 2

20g/¾ oz butter, cut into small cubes
25g/1 oz light muscovado sugar
2 tbsp golden syrup
3 tbsp double cream
2 large bananas

1. Put the butter, sugar, syrup and cream into a small bowl and stir well. Cover with foil, crimping the edges securely against the sides of the bowl.

2. Put the bowl into the steamer and lay the whole bananas alongside.

3. Cover with the lid and steam for 12-15 minutes until the bananas are brown and soft and are just starting to split open.

4. With a small whisk, stir the sauce until blended and smooth.

5. Carefully lift the bananas on to serving plates. Make a slit along each one, pulling back the skin gently. Drizzle the bananas with some sauce and serve the rest separately.

Spiced Rhubarb with Orange

Here the rhubarb, which keeps its shape beautifully, is flavoured with orange and a subtle hint of spices. Serve it with sponge fingers. It tastes even nicer if you leave it (with the spices) overnight in the refrigerator.

Serves 4

450g/1 lb rhubarb, cut into 2.5cm/1 in lengths
finely grated rind and juice of 1 medium orange
85g/3 oz caster sugar
1 cinnamon stick
3 whole cloves

1. Combine all the ingredients until well mixed and put into a bowl large enough to fit the steamer. Cover with foil, crimping the edges securely against the sides.

2. Put the bowl into the steamer and cover with the lid. Steam for about 40 minutes or until the rhubarb is tender.

3. Remove the cinnamon stick and cloves before serving warm or chilled.

Pears with Chocolate Sauce

Fruit and chocolate – everyone's favourite combination! For a really rich sauce, use chocolate with at least 50% cocoa solids.

Serves 4

4 firm, ripe pears
1 lemon
125g/4½ oz plain chocolate
2 tbsp maple syrup or golden syrup
15g/½ oz butter
1 tbsp brandy, rum or orange liqueur (optional)

1. Peel the pears, leaving the stalks intact. Halve the lemon and rub one half over the outside of the pears.

2. Stand the pears in the steamer and cover with the lid. Steam for 20 minutes.

3. Meanwhile, chop the chocolate and put it into a bowl. Add the syrup and butter. Squeeze the juice from the remaining lemon half and add 2 tsp to the chocolate mixture. Cover the dish with foil, crimping the edges securely to the sides.

4. Add the dish to the second steamer tier and replace the lid. Continue steaming the pears and chocolate mixture for about 10 minutes or until the pears are soft and the chocolate has melted.

5. Stir the sauce until smooth and glossy. If using, stir in the brandy, rum or orange liqueur. Serve the pears with the sauce spooned over them.

Bread and Butter Pudding

I was quite surprised that this recipe worked so well in the steamer. The resulting pudding is light and creamy and the sugar and cinnamon topping makes up for the lack of crispy edges. Try using different bread if you prefer, such as a French stick or a fruit loaf.

Serves 4

butter
6 slices of bread
50g/1¾ oz dried fruit, such as sultanas, raisins, chopped dates or chopped ready-to-eat apricots
2 large eggs
1 tsp vanilla extract
40g/1½ oz caster sugar, plus 2 tsp
450ml/16 fl oz milk
150ml/¼ pt double cream
¼ tsp ground cinnamon

1. Lightly butter a dish that will fit in the steamer (a soufflé dish works well). Butter the bread on one side and cut each slice into quarters. Lay the bread, overlapping in the dish, scattering the dried fruit over and between.

2. Beat the eggs with the vanilla and the 40g/1½ oz sugar.

3. Heat the milk and cream in a pan (or in the microwave for 2-3 minutes) until hot but not boiling. Gradually whisk it into the eggs. Strain the mixture over the bread and leave to stand for about 30 minutes so that the bread soaks up the liquid.

4. Put the uncovered dish into the steamer and cover with the lid. Steam for about 30 minutes or until just set at the centre (the pudding will rise up quite high during steaming and then settle again once cooking is completed).

5. Leave to stand for 5-10 minutes before serving, then mix the remaining 2 tsp sugar with the cinnamon and sprinkle over the top of the pudding. Serve immediately.

Chinese Steamed Cake

Steaming gives this typical Chinese cake a light and fluffy texture. Cook it either in a bamboo steamer lined with baking paper or, as I do, in a soufflé dish. Serve it warm with vanilla ice cream or with softly whipped cream flavoured with some chopped preserved ginger and a spoonful of its juice.

Serves 4-6

3 large eggs, separated
140g/5 oz caster sugar
100ml/3½ fl oz single cream
1 tsp vanilla extract
finely grated rind of 1 lemon
85g/3 oz butter, melted and cooled
150g/5½ oz self-raising flour
1 tsp baking powder
pinch of salt

1. Butter a 20cm/8 in soufflé dish (check that it will fit in the steamer) and line the base with baking paper.

2. Whisk together the egg yolks and sugar until thick and creamy. Whisk in the cream, vanilla, lemon rind and butter. Sift the flour, baking powder and salt over the top and stir in.

3. In a clean bowl and with clean beaters, whisk the egg whites until soft peaks are formed. Using a metal spoon, fold into the cake mixture (it should be well mixed but try not to knock out too much air). Gently tip the mixture into the prepared dish.

4. Put the uncovered dish into the steamer and cover with the lid. Steam for 20-25 minutes or until a skewer inserted deep in the centre of the cake comes out clean.

5. Leave to stand for 5 minutes before carefully turning the cake out of the dish and removing the paper.

Coconut Creams with Mango

Serve with dainty crisp biscuits, such as amaretti – it's a good idea to crumble one on top of each serving.

Serves 4

200ml carton coconut cream
200ml double cream
finely grated rind of 1 lime or lemon
50g/1¾ oz caster sugar
4 medium eggs, beaten
1 large ripe mango, peeled, stone removed and chopped

1. Pour the coconut cream and double cream into a small saucepan, add the lime rind and sugar and heat gently, stirring, until the sugar has dissolved (alternatively heat in the microwave for about 2 minutes, stirring once or twice). Leave to cool slightly.

2. Lightly whisk the eggs, then whisk in the coconut mixture. Pour into four small dishes or ramekins.

3. Put the uncovered dishes in the steamer and cover with the lid. Steam for about 10 minutes or until the custards are just.

4. Leave to cool, then chill for 1-2 hours.

5. Serve topped with the fresh mango.

10
PARCELS AND WRAPS

I just love to cook food in parcels or wrapped in leaves – there is always a slight element of surprise when it comes to serving them and everyone enjoys finding out what's inside. Parcels and wraps are really convenient too because they can usually be prepared in advance, ready for steaming just when you need them. So just in case you are as enthusiastic as I am, here is a quick list of suitable recipes and where they are to be found in the book.

INDEX